This timely book provides *the* definite concise introduction to the phenomenon of Zygmunt Bauman. After introducing the man, his major influences and his special way of 'thinking sociologically', Blackshaw traces the development of Bauman's project by identifying and explaining the major shifts of emphasis in his work – the break with Marxism and the postmodern 'turn' and the subsequent refocusing on 'liquid' modernity – as well as offering a clear and accessible guide to the key conceptual hinges which move the reader from one to the other.

The book goes on to explain the importance of the full range of persistent themes concerning Bauman, dealing specifically with individualization, freedom, identity, community, social control, consumption and waste, building a penetrating understanding of why these issues matter for this *Key Sociologist*.

The book assumes no prior familiarity with Bauman's work and will appeal to anyone wishing to get acquainted with the ideas of one of the world's most wide-ranging thinkers.

Tony Blackshaw is Senior Lecturer in Sociology at Sheffield Hallam University. He has recently completed two major studies in the sociology of sport and leisure – *New Perspective on Sport and 'Deviance': Consumption, Performativity and Social Control* (co-authored) (2004) and *Leisure Life: Myth, Masculinity and Modernity* (2003), both published by Routledge.

ZYGMUNT BAUMAN

TONY BLACKSHAW

LONDON AND NEW YORK

First published 2005
by Routledge
2 Park Square, Milton Park, Abingdon, Oxon OX14 4RN

Simultaneously published in the USA and Canada
by Routledge
270 Madison Ave, New York, NY 10016

Routledge is an imprint of the Taylor & Francis Group

Typeset in Times by
HWA Text and Data Management Ltd, Tunbridge Wells
Printed and bound in Great Britain by
TJ International Ltd, Padstow, Cornwall

British Library Cataloguing in Publication Data
A catalogue record for this book is available from the British
Library

Library of Congress Cataloging in Publication Data
Blackshaw, Tony, 1960–
　Zygmunt Bauman / by Tony Blackshaw
　　　p. cm. – (Key sociologists)
　Includes bibliographical references and index.
　1. Bauman, Zygmunt. 2. Sociology. 3. Postmodernism–Social
　aspects. I. Title. II. Series: Key sociologists (Routledge (Firm))
　HM479.B39B53 2005
　301′.092–dc22　　　　　　　　　　　　　2005000371

ISBN 0–415–35505–2 (hbk)
ISBN 0–415–35504–4 (pbk)

For my Mam and Dad, who, for better and for worse, have found it more sincere to live their lives wearing steel casings rather than light cloaks

Table of Contents

Preface

For all the shape-shifting qualities its major protagonists have brought to the discipline over the years, the ability to break with the orthodoxy in sociology has always been a rare commodity and most sociologists slot comfortably into a lineage, recalling others who have gone before. Indeed, today the discipline continues to be sustained by its ready-made 'isms', which acquire their own aesthetics, marking their protagonists as compellingly as that death-in-life zombie category[1] of social class used to divide up the totality in its 'solid' modern stage: Marxists, symbolic interactionists, ethnomethodologists, figurationalists, feminists and the more freshly-minted postmodernists and poststructuralists and the rest. It takes someone both imaginative and brave to shake off the dust of heritage, duck fashion, and try to do their own thing, but Zygmunt Bauman is that kind of sociologist. As the reader will find out in the course of following chapters, nobody has the heart and passion that Bauman has for his sociology and this is what gives him confidence to break the mould.

To say that Bauman stands out among his contemporaries is not the same as saying that his work is altogether distinctive, though; on the contrary, he is a figure whose sociology represents a dialogue between many strands of social thought. As I demonstrate in this book, one of the more explicit intellectual lineages in Bauman's sociology is the one with the anti-establishment perspective of Richard Rorty, who argues for new and innovative ways of writing about the world. Like Rorty, Bauman recognizes that there is no reason why sociologists shouldn't be creative writers and in so doing he develops his own 'talent for speaking differently'. In this regard, Bauman finds meaning in the sorts of places most professors of sociology are not prepared to look, for example, in films such as *The Exorcist* and *The Omen*, 'reality' TV shows like *Big Brother* and even in soap operas like *Eastenders*.

Bauman is also like Rorty in another way in that he is not concerned with establishing whether there is or isn't a 'real' world in his sociology. He simply recognizes that if sociologists want to argue convincingly for new ways of understanding the world, they must recognize that they cannot resort to any foundational criteria for justifying that their version of that world is better than anybody else's. In other words, they can do nothing else in their analyses but simply assume that there is something like an already existing reality and get on with the task of getting to grips with it.

There is however a very important difference between what Bauman and Rorty do. Whereas Rorty merely offers us intimations of a *modernist way of theorizing*, Bauman produces in his work *a new theory of modernity*.[2] And in so doing he realizes for the reader of sociology that most difficult of tasks: he conjures up a critical analysis of modernity in such a way as to make it pulse. This is because sociology remains for Bauman one of the most extraordinary tools available for social change and like Marx before him his work is implicitly critical of philosophers like Rorty who 'so far have only interpreted the world in various ways; the point is to change it'.[3]

Bauman became a sociologist because he wants to change the world and in this regard his sociology is first and foremost an extended critique of modernity. But it is also a critique of modernity that if it recognizes that 'no single-factor model is likely ever to account for the complexity of the "lived world" and embrace the totality of human experience',[4] it acknowledges too that as a result of extended processes of globalization, modernity is a much smaller place than it used to be. Bauman's is a sociology that also recognizes that if in global terms the gap between the rich and poor has grown much larger over the last twenty-five years – and continues to do so – it concedes that the struggles that people have to endure to make a decent life for themselves are both the same and yet different from what they were in the past. In this sense Bauman's is a critique of modernity that knows that if for many of those eking out an existence in the so-called 'developing' world the struggle is business as usual, it is prepared to acknowledge that, for men and women living in the bloated consumerist economies of the West, inequality has changed in ways unimaginable only twenty or thirty years ago.

In all of these senses Bauman's is a sociology which, if it is not prepared to accept poverty and social exclusion, is acutely aware of the likely ambivalences facing any critique of modernity today. Bauman knows that if we want to change the world for the better we must not only come to terms with the fact that human misery exists because of economic, political and social inequalities but also recognize it exists because men and women are in the main still reluctant to look for the many and different kinds of ambivalence implicit in modernity – including the ambivalences within their own lives and the ideologies with which they are bolstered – rather they would for the most part close their eyes to these and more than likely project the bases of them onto the lives of others. Those familiar with Marx, or even Hegel, will say that Bauman is merely redescribing the dialectic here, but that would be to misunderstand his brilliant point that *ambivalence* is the creature of modernity, and people's lives today more than any time in the past are governed by the contingency of events.

If not going as far as saying that the 'liquid' modernity we today inhabit is a world where 'anything goes', Bauman reminds us that we share a 'lighter, diffuse and more mobile' sociality where there is no one set of constraints, no definitive set of rules. A liquid modernity in which people's lives are indelibly stamped with ambivalence and where routine,

> the habits it requires, and the learning that results in both, do not pay any longer. In a fluid setting, flexibility is the name of rationality. Skills do not retain usefulness for long, for what was yesterday a masterstroke may prove today inane or downright suicidal. Just as long-term commitments threaten to mortgage the future, habits too tightly embraced burden the present; learning may in the long run disempower as it empowers in the short.[5]

Bauman once said that 'to claim the right to speak with authority, sociology would have to update its theory of society'[6] and what I want to argue in this book is that in developing his own sociology of the sociality of 'liquid' modernity Bauman has concentrated on this as his central task. My foremost intention in writing the book is to demonstrate that what we get with Bauman is the extent of contemporary human life of which sociology is capable of depicting; and not only that, but a full range of new theories, ideas and concepts to boot, which enhance our 'talent for speaking differently' about the world.

The book is divided into five chapters but it is different to most other *Key Sociologists* books in that it does not consciously present Bauman's ideas in the order they developed. Rather the book is on the one hand a primer, in the sense that it deals with what is essential and constitutive with understanding Bauman and what he has had to say about understanding the contemporary world, and on the other it offers a critique which draws on these insights to say something about the important ways in which Bauman's sociology connects with the hermeneutic relationship between the quotidian and mainstream sociology. As the reader will see, this second aspect runs as a thread throughout the book.

If the first chapter provides only a bare bones sketch of Bauman's biographical details, it offers a much more thoroughgoing discussion of the man in relation to his special way of 'thinking sociologically'. In this regard it also confronts head on the major confusions and misconceptions that surround Bauman's sociology as well as dealing with the problematic of exploring the work of a thinker whose ideas contain no lesson plans in their arrangement. As the reader will see, Bauman does not run with any sociological pack and what he offers by the way of sociological perspective is neither a systematic elaboration of interconnected theoretical themes nor something that could be described as a school of thought.

Chapter 2 builds on the foregoing analysis by outlining and discussing both the diachronic and the synchronic development of Bauman's sociology from the mid-1980s onwards. In this regard it deals with the circumstances of Bauman's break with Marxism as well as outlining his theory of modernity. In the process of developing these two interrelated analyses, the chapter also highlights the major shifts of emphasis in Bauman's work. I suggest two particular moments which any introductory reader of Bauman must consider: his 'postmodern' turn and the replacement of the preliminary and 'negative' concept of postmodernity with the 'positive' concept of liquid modernity.

Chapter 3 argues that if Bauman himself has had little to say about issues of methodology, the ways and means of his sociology tell quite a different story. In offering this critique I draw on Bauman's theory of modernity to argue that contemporary sociology is characteristically conservative and corrective and that it can only be transformed once it begins to contemplate itself: when it is prepared to come to terms with its own impossibility and consciously discard what it has unconsciously been doing since its inception. It is suggested that with its literary heartbeat Bauman's sociology provides a compelling challenge to the sociological hegemony which still operates on the basis that without its orthodox theory and empirical evidence continuum the discipline cannot persist.

In the second part of Chapter 3 it is argued that Bauman makes both culture and hermeneutics central to the task of 'thinking sociologically' and in this regard I explore in some detail his crucial lesson for sociology, which is that if there are no ready-made guidelines for how we are supposed to do sociology, this does not mean to say that our sociologies cannot be all at once rigorous, poetic and ethical in their quest to contemplate the already existing reality in all its quotidian untidiness. In extending the theme of the ethical requirements of a sociology made to the measure of liquid modern times, the final section of the chapter argues that, for Bauman, if sociology in its formative years was too preoccupied with the circumstances of conformity, obedience and consensus making, the challenge facing it today is the matter of choice between assuming *responsibility* and engaging in the struggle for what is good for humankind or *bystanding* and therefore choosing not to act.

Freedom and security are the two poles between which all Bauman's sociology is strung. And it is his central argument that in liquid modernity security has waned towards more freedom and this has resulted in men's and women's lives increasingly taking on the imprint of individualization. In developing Bauman's idea that DIY individual identity seeking is today our fate, in Chapter 4 I extend my discussion of the ways and means of his sociology to demonstrate how it challenges the organization of human culture within the academy to offer a form of analysis which, if it is not social psychological in orientation, it is, following Sartre and to a lesser extent Freud, guided by a method of existential psychoanalysis. In order to develop the reader's understanding of the implications of the swing towards more freedom and individualization, I also make some critical comparisons between Bauman's sociology and that of Bourdieu. Thereafter I discuss the theme of identity in some depth before considering Bauman's argument that the extent and the style of liquid modern freedoms weigh heavily on individual shoulders and it is no wonder men and women spend a good deal of their time trying to find some security in community.

The fifth and final chapter of the book explores in some detail Bauman's argument that liquid modernity is a time when men's and women's freedom depends on their ability to consume. After exploring the aesthetical, political and ethical implications of consumerism for freedom, I consider Bauman's argument that consumerism has major implications for explaining patterns of social control in liquid modernity. In this regard I show that Foucault's Panopticon model of social control no longer holds good and that social control, like much else in liberal democracies, has by and large been commodified and privatized. The final part of the chapter once again returns to the theme of the implications of liquid modernity for sociology. The discussion here considers Bauman's argument that intellectual work like other commodities for sale in liquid modernity increasingly comes in two modalities: one that embraces the flash trash of consumer culture and another which seeks refuge from consumerism in a dash for heritage and nostalgia in the sociology of the founding fathers. The book ends with the thought that if liquid modernity is a time when authenticity is so uncompromisingly sought but rarely found, what we have in Bauman is a man who not only manages to write challenging and important books, but who in each and every one of them seems to make sociology more essential than it ever has been.

1

An Interim Career Report

Zygmunt Bauman will be 80 years young this year and in this book I want to argue that, while he took longer than his contemporaries to make his mark, he not only stayed the course but also became the sociology-sovereign of his generation. No sociologist writing today, not one that I know of, not one, is more in touch with the *Zeitgeist* than Bauman. When I first studied sociology in the late 1980s, Anthony Giddens was generally understood as the most important sociologist in the English-speaking world. However, it is without any hesitation that I suggest that Bauman has not only now replaced him, but in the process has also become twenty-first century sociology's foremost interpreter, its professor of professors.

This urbane, pipe-smoking sociologist is older than Giddens but the significance of his work in the academy was initially much slower in coming. His career evolved, gathering momentum as it went along. The evidence of Blackwell's and Polity Press's back catalogues shows that Bauman really found his stride after his 'retirement' from the University of Leeds in 1990, and so too did his approach to sociology, which he has incrementally been developing with every new publication in what has become nothing less than a stupendous output: books on topics such as modernity, the Holocaust, postmodernity, liquid modernity, freedom, consumer culture, death and life strategies, globalization, poverty, community, love, waste, identity and Europe. If Bauman can't write about everything that is to do with how we live now, it seems as if he's saying 'it won't be for the want of me trying'.

If there was an award for ubiquity, Bauman would win it hands down. To this day he continues to maintain a punishing pace of academic activity, more often than not publishing two or three books in a year, or so it seems. Over and above that, he keeps on turning out essays and reviews for journals, edited collections, and newspapers as well as accepting countless invitations for interviews and to present to university departments and conferences around the globe. He might write with the speed of a Las Vegas card dealer shuffling his pack but for all their regularity Bauman's publications are always arduous, subtle and prolonged exercises in the sociological imagination. Bauman subverts a truism in sociology, because with his tremendous output it is not less, but actually more that is more. Indeed what is impressive about Bauman's project is how rigorously his ideas continue to be sustained.

The words 'sociologist' and 'superstar' rarely come together, but what other combination would you use to describe a sociologist who is by now a global phenomenon – world sociology's most convincing and authoritative voice – and who for a decade has been firmly established in his role as *the* chronicler *par excellence* of modernity, as well as being *the* major exponent and developer of social theory writing during the same period. For his growing band of followers, there is no doubt that Bauman is a superstar. The man himself would reject such a label not least because of its implications – Bauman is an intellectual, complete, uncompromising in his rejection of the pop and pap that comes with celebrity; his eye is not on any audience for his work but set on interpreting *and* trying to change for the better the multitudinous world that we today inhabit, and he's got his finger right on its pulse.

Theoretically gifted but with real-world know-how, the Polish-born sociologist emerges in this book as an accomplished intellectual of more talent than genius. It is the ability to universalize that distinguishes the best sociology and Bauman's is a universal remedy to awaken the sleeping sociologist in all of us. The writing is as fluent as the analyses of the contemporary world are compelling and to this extent Bauman is that novelty in British sociology: somebody who can write. But what is even more startling is that he is an exemplary writer in English despite the fact that it is not his first language. He isn't a sociologist in any conventional sense either. As a writer of sociology Bauman has a special skill for telling stories – not many sociologists are good story-tellers. Having said that, to the uninitiated, the writing style can appear difficult, and for a moment seem out of touch with the quotidian, the *Zeitgeist* and what

Bauman himself calls its 'mechanism and momentum'. But if the reader persists they will find that Bauman's is in fact straightforwardly the most 'in tune' sociology there is and will see that his concerns and ideas that leap from the countless pages are intense and fascinating, but also disturbingly immediate and pressing.

Like the world he depicts in the pages of his books, Bauman's sociology is constantly in flux, and to employ a metaphor from Egyptian mythology, it's as if since his 'retirement' he has been intent on changing the orthodox sociological template by turning around the Isis and Osiris fable. If orthodox sociology was his Osiris, Bauman began to cut it into pieces for resisting the changing contemporary world around it, while we, his Isis, began to search for sociology after him, picking up each fragment that we found in his new writings in order to give our own sociological imaginations a new part and a purpose.

Indeed, Bauman's sociology, like all other living art, is always on the move; it is a work that is always in progress; it is a work of interlocking parts and these parts are in constant movement. To wish for an unchanging Bauman would be to wish for an obsessive more than a thinker who is always prepared to engage with new ideas. To read his work is also to be moved by the grace of his sentences, the ease of his wit, the suppleness of his narrative thread and the complexity and inventiveness of his ideas. For the work to be fixedly consistent would also deny its power as the most powerful record of modern life, with all that that entails: anxiety, uncertainty, risk, fragmentation, contingency and ambivalence. Bauman's work is in the Enlightenment sense a meticulous project, but it is so in a way that is not unmediated by its author's imperfections, a grandiose scheme of work sabotaged by the liquid ambivalence of the ideas of its own mastermind.

The ability to take a subject we all thought we knew and to turn our taken-for-granted assumptions about it on their heads with common sense as well as painstaking scholarship, is the mark of Bauman's sociology. To paraphrase that most perceptive of social commentators, Roland Barthes, Bauman follows the dictum that knowledge is coarse, life is subtle, and sociology matters because it corrects this distance. Indeed, Bauman turns the rhythms of everyday life into an erudite and critical practice that burns itself into the sociological imagination. Most of us perhaps recognize many of the themes that Bauman deals with in his sociology, but he is a master of bringing them into narratives about real people and their lives. The hinges which take us from one book to the next are always themes of the most pressing kind – freedom, security, responsibility, poverty, love, identity, community – which hold a deep and continuing resonance for their author and his readers.

POINTS OF EMPHASIS

This book signals a new direction in Bauman studies. It parts company with the other key introductions, such as Dennis Smith's (1999) *Zygmunt Bauman: Prophet of Postmodernity*, Peter Beilharz's (2000) *Zygmunt Bauman: Dialectic of Modernity* and Keith Tester's (2004) *The Social Thought of Zygmunt Bauman*, each of which follow a similar intellectual trajectory by mapping Bauman's project, chronologically, from his Marxist beginnings, throughout his 'postmodern' turn to the emergence in his writings of the idea of liquid modernity. Although each of these books more than ably addresses many of the topics, issues and concepts that concern Bauman, they each rely too heavily on the notion that Bauman's key ideas will speak for themselves if they are presented in sufficient detail. In this sense they collectively fail to place Bauman's special way of going about sociology in a context which is accessible to undergraduates and other readers who are not conversant in social theory. This is a book which if it is critical in its focus it is not so polemical as to forget the interests and needs of the reader who is coming to Bauman for the first time, or who wants step-by-step guidance.

In order to achieve my own objective of making Bauman more accessible, in the main I steer clear of the chronology and the content of his major book-length studies where the typical mode of narration involves too much excursus and the backdrops for the analyses often feature Greek mythology and Biblical metaphors. Bauman wants to challenge his readers but for the uninitiated these books are too densely packed with esoteric vocabulary and foreign – mostly German – terms as well, and the sentences, like the paragraphs and chapters, are often long, meandering and at times as difficult to unravel as a Gordian knot. If not wilfully obscure, some of these books are difficult to understand not merely because of the intricacy of the ideas, theories, themes and concepts which Bauman endeavours to express in his writing, but also because of their sheer scope, which encompasses a massive range of erudition. Moreover his wanting his readers to hold on to ideas previously developed in his work, such as, for example, the ambivalence of modernity, means that he is not the easiest of social theorists to grasp. So rather than trying to cut the knot with Alexander's sword, for the most part I try to develop the discussion with Bauman's most accessible work, which means the interviews and the more recent publications published in Polity's *Themes for the 21st Century* series. The direct quotations used are almost always drawn from interviews too, which provide the reader with a Bauman that, if he is not as precise as the one found in his more essayistic book publications, is much more welcoming.

Readers will find in this book then an alternative way of understanding Bauman, its purpose not being to provide yet another rendition of the writings to what is ostensibly a professorial audience, so much as a guide for the introductory reader, designed to shed some light on the scope of his sociological vision. With this objective in mind, I knew from the outset that if I was going to be successful I would have to put in sufficient spadework so as to get into the head of my subject. Bauman was my own discovery of perspective – he gave me a kind of sociology I could think with – and as the project developed it became more and more evident to me that if I was going to be really successful in getting a sense of this across to my readers, I would not only have to demonstrate that I have the appropriate sociological imagination to look at the world through Bauman's eyes, but also that I would have the ability to convey something of the extent of the inimitable possibilities of that experience. The reader will of course be the judge of my success in fulfilling this purpose.

SOME MISCONCEPTIONS ABOUT BAUMAN

I reasoned that this approach would also allow me to deal with the commentaries that board but do not capture Bauman's work and which as a result are often ambiguous, contradictory and in places simply inaccurate. As a consequence, a great cloud of fame seems to surround his name in sociology today but within it there are too many pockets of obscurity. As Peter Beilharz[1] has pointed out, just as 'Gramsci was reinvented by local radicals as an Englishman via the work of the Birmingham School', so some equally energetic but misconceived interpreters have locked Bauman in a triumvirate with Anthony Giddens and Ulrich Beck. However, there are two more basic and equally serious misconceptions about Bauman that I need to deal with before this introduction can proceed. The first is that he is a postmodernist and the second is that in his analyses he puts too much emphasis on the individual-ization of everyday life.

Bauman, postmodernity and postmodernism

The idea that Bauman is a postmodernist is a misconception made most particularly in three camps: those who dismiss him and don't get past the front covers of his books, those who find his work too difficult to under-stand, and/or those who fail to read him carefully and misrepresent his views. The reader needs to grasp from the outset that Bauman is *not* a postmodernist in the negative use of the concept and he never has been. However, they need to be aware that Bauman has always cast his net wide in developing the many avenues of new inquiry pursued in his sociology and he has been influenced a great deal by thinkers whose work has been described as postmodern in orientation.

In understanding the relationship between the work of these thinkers and Bauman's own, it is instructive to consider the career of the term 'modernity' in the sociology literature. Sociologists only first began talking about the idea of modernity as a concept of significance in the late 1980s. Evidence for this can be found in the dictionaries and specialist glossaries of the time. For example, in Raymond Williams's (1983) revised edition of *Keywords* (London: Fontana) there is barely any recognition of 'modernity', other than it being a derivative of the word 'modern', whereas there are a full nine pages devoted to 'social class'. Sociologists only really started to talk about the idea of modernity with the emergence of theories of postmodernism and from this point modernity merged into a dialectic (modernism in opposition to postmodernism and modernity in opposition to postmodernity), and the concept achieved a new independence. As Keith Tester[2] points out, in his own analyses Bauman borrowed the idea of the distinction between modernity and postmodernity from the work of the architect Charles Jencks and when he

> took up discussion about the postmodern, [but] inevitably he shifted the context of the word. He took the aesthetics of postmodern*ism* and turned it, instead, into an inspiration and competent part of a sociology of postmodernity. In these terms, postmodern*ism* is about aesthetics and artistic production, whereas postmodernity, 'refers to a distinct quality of intellectual climate, to a distinctly new meta-cultural stance, to a distinct self-awareness of the era'.[3]

In defining postmodernity in these terms, Bauman's arguments differed fundamentally from postmodernism,[4] which postulates the argument that it is the infinite questioning of rationality that leads to the demise of the 'grand narrative' of modernity. It is the postmodern view that, in trying to find the ultimate truth, in seeking ground for its knowledge, rationality unavoidably lays the foundations for its own destruction. In this postmodern world, it is rationality that produces nihility, which is the ultimate consequence of hyper-rationality. And once rationality has been banished from the 'business of life', there can no longer be any single objective reality, nor any observation that is not merely postulation; what we have is nothing more than 'the play of signifiers … in which the code[5] no longer refers back to any subjective or objective "reality", but to its own logic'.[6] Postmodernism's postmodernity is a depthless, hyperized asociality, where individual agency is irrelevant and which gives priority to the 'code' over subjective ideas and in the process marks the victory of the 'anti-social sign over the social sign'.[7]

The view Bauman developed suggested that, contrary to Baudrillard's postmodernism, rationality and social agency still inspire the enthusiasm and enticement for the good life in postmodernity, but they are guided by a 'will to happiness' which is progressively more individualized and social relationships are increasingly lifted out of their more traditional contexts to form new *habitats*, which 'unbind' time and weaken the coercive impact of the past,[8] a process which Bauman has described, using one of Giddens's metaphors, as 'the continuation of disembedding coupled with dis-continuation of re-embedding'.[9] In a nutshell, with postmodernity life was increasingly coming to be experienced as discontinuous, more comparable to a collection of moments or a series of episodes, which are 'constantly in-the-state-of-becoming, unfinished and revocable ... [and] eminently "dismantlable"'.[10] In this way Bauman's interpretation of postmodernity had more in common with Lyotard's more concise definition of postmodernism, which suggested that this shift in modernity involved a rejection of all grand narratives, or big stories, for new ways of living that undermined the old 'certainist' ways of life associated with modernity.

George Ritzer is to a large extent correct in suggesting that Bauman's sociology of postmodernity is continuous with classical sociology in its strategy of providing both systematic and rational accounts of the social world.[11] However, Ritzer overlooks the point that Bauman is also ambivalent towards classical sociology. For in his role as the postmodern interpreter, Bauman remains unconvinced of any sociology that is based on purely systematic thought, rationality and reason; notions which, for Bauman, must always be understood as the slaves of difference.

It should be understood that Bauman's sociology of postmodernity draws on orthodox sociological accounts, but as I will demonstrate in the following pages it also draws on a broad range of thinking, including social philosophy, hermeneutics, cultural studies, literature, post-structuralism and especially postmodern understandings to develop extant sociological theories to help to understand the profound changes under-lying our contemporary social condition. Despite the obvious advantages of the vocabulary of postmodern sociology, though, Bauman also recognizes its limited utility for social analysis in that it 'denies its kinship with a specific stage in the history of social life'.[12] Bauman's key point is that by re-imagining sociology as a *sociology of postmodernity* we are able to overcome the limitations of *postmodern sociology* because we do not overlook the problem of social structure in relation to the nature of large-scale socio-historical transformations, and the role of individual actors within these processes.[13]

For postmodernists of Baudrillard's persuasion, Bauman's sociology might be conceived as merely an affirmation and preservation of an outdated modern enterprise, but by acknowledging clearly that sociology must come to terms with the ways in which the world has changed around it, Bauman offers an extraordinary way to re-interpret and assimilate the most useful of some 'older' sociological postulations with 'new' theoretical insights to make sense of these new times. Very simply, Bauman allows us to see more, facilitating the sort of thoroughgoing interpretation that is only achieved when the world is 'read' from different perspectives. If, for Bauman himself, Georg Simmel is the unsung pioneer of the sociology of postmodernity,[14] then he is its current inspiration, the 'new' main man, the funky jazz master-mixer of the new millennium.

If Bauman was one of the first major sociologists to write extensively and affirmingly on the topic of postmodernity and he was once unhesitant about describing and theorizing postmodernity in an open way, a certain reticence in this connection has appeared in his most recent writings. He now prefers the terms 'solid' modernity and 'liquid' modernity as opposed to 'modernity' and 'postmodernity'. With the switch to liquid modernity and solid modernity as opposed to postmodernity and modernity, another kind of soundtrack – a sociology *after* postmodernism – began to soar and throb behind Bauman's rhythmic prose.

It should be stressed however that this change in focus merely marks a tactical shift in Bauman's work. Indeed, the ideas of freedom and responsibility remain as ever the cornerstones of his critical project. This shift in emphasis should really come as no surprise to us, however, given the irrepressible proliferation of discourses on the idea of the postmodern which have emerged in recent years. Theoreticians – often diametrically opposed – have seemed determined to outbid each other in their zeal to reveal the 'truth' about the postmodern, rendering the term almost devoid of any critical use value. Having said that, the reader needs to be aware that to properly get to grips with Bauman's project requires more than a fair degree of engagement with postmodernism and the work of a range of postmodern theorists and I will be returning to these throughout the book.

The individual and 'society'

The second major misconception that is railed against in this book is the idea that in his sociology Bauman puts too much emphasis on individuals and processes of individualization at the expense of focusing his attention on contemporary social formations and latter-day forms of community. In the words of Bauman himself, responding to this criticism of his sociology:

> In liquid-modern society we all, and each one of us, are instructed … to seek biographical exits from the socially concocted mess. So we are all individuals by (unwritten) decree – spending most of our life trying to gain an individuality *de facto*. This is a tall order of a task, and no wonder we tend to dream of respite. It is not true that I focus on individualisation 'at the expense' of togetherness – it is my belief that, in fact, they cannot be discussed, let alone grasped, separately. I have written a little book on community with a subtitle 'seeking safety in an uncertain world'. The more lonely we feel, the more we speak of community (which invariably stands for slowing down in the world of mind-boggling acceleration); but community is at its strongest when it can stay silent and can do without self-adulation. The world in which community (as Raymond Williams put it) is 'always has been', the gaping void is hastily filled by what I call 'peg communities', 'ad hoc communities', 'explosive communities' and other disposable substitutes meant for an instant and one-off consumption … They quench the thirst for security, albeit briefly. None is likely to deliver on the hopes invested, since they leave the roots of insecurity unscathed.[15]

We can discern from this quotation that if Bauman's allegiance augers on the side of the individual it is first and foremost because of his respect for cultural difference. For that reason he is also sceptical of any notion if it implies essentialism.

This is why he is scathing of the strategic essentialism associated with communitarianism. However, this does not make him a liberal individualist – the philosophical position which is usually cast as the binary opposite of communitarianism. Liberal individualists are content to understand the individual 'free' to make choices as an essentially autonomous agent. For Bauman, it is democracy that is the ultimate guarantor of individual freedom, not the other way round. Indeed, as the reader would expect, Bauman's approach is a thoroughgoing sociological understanding of freedom, which recognizes that freedom is always a social relation. As Ian Varcoe has suggested, for Bauman, social relations 'are already hardened into an established social reality, to which the actor must adapt or adjust'.[16] What is more, for Bauman, as for Martin Heidegger, our individual 'being in the world' is always 'being with others' and he starts from the assumption that the individual agent cannot be imagined, let alone talked about alone; social action should not be understood as taking place in a vacuum or 'starting from scratch';[17] that human lives are lived together is a given, because they are by necessity built on social relations. In other words, for Bauman, structure and agency leap together.

Against the reified determinism of modernist sociological perspectives such as structural-functionalism and orthodox Marxism, Bauman argues that 'structures emerge from the far end of culture's struggle. They stand for the "inevitable", only to be eroded and in the end folded up, cut into pieces and dissolved by the culture's indefatigable and intransigent rebelliousness, pugnacity and swagger.'[18] It is culture rather than structure which makes humanity the 'permanent revolution' that it is. Bauman also invokes a structure–agency dialectic whose watchword might be 'all power to the subject'. His is a kind of sociology which in favouring agency over structure also favours everyday-language conceptions – freedom, respect, responsibility, love and so on and so forth – as opposed to the compulsory intellectual terminology found in many sociological accounts. Bauman's work is thus suggestive of a sociology that is better suited to people's everyday lives, while being attentive to the point that some people 'are freer than others, some in being free in effect structure the world *for* others'.[19]

This last point notwithstanding, what Bauman is bringing to our attention in his sociology is what is different about contemporary social relations, which is that individualization is becoming the *social structure of second modernity* [liquid modernity] *itself.*[20] As he explains:

> It does not matter whether single men and women have become genuinely more autonomous, more 'on their own', more determined by their own choices and actions as before; what does matter is that they are now charged with full responsibility for their false or ill-conceived steps, failures or defeats – and that they confront the kind of problems whose chance of resolution would not gain much from joining forces and acting in common. As Ulrich Beck memorably put it, each of us is now expected to seek [individual] biographical solutions to socially produced troubles.[21]

Bauman sees liquid modernity not so much as a world of egocentric individuals who shape their lives as personal projects made through their own imaginings about the possibilities that the world out there has to offer, but one in which men and women are reflective moral agents who live in an uncertain world which means that they are forced in the quotidian of their day-to-day lives to contemplate their existential insecurities. Bauman's sociology, more than any other written today, recognizes that if social actors are busy getting on with the business of life it is because they are very much aware that as individuals – *de jure* if not *de facto* – they have no choice but to try to reach some sort of completeness and order in their lives out of all the in-betweens with which they are confronted so that they can make some sort of sense of the world in all its contingent excess.

REPRESENTING BAUMAN

The reader should also be aware from the outset that there have been two Zygmunt Bauman's: Mark One, a cultural Marxist sociologist, who died a slow death; and the second, Mark Two version – the concern of this book – who rose out of the shroud of the first Bauman. In relation to this rebirth and as I have already intimated above, there are two particular moments which any introductory reader of Bauman must consider: his 'postmodern' turn and the replacement of what he has described as the preliminary and 'negative' concept of postmodernity with the 'positive' concept of liquid modernity. It is my proposition that from the publication of *Legislators and Interpreters* onwards there is a move in Bauman's sociology which has the effect of a parallax; the perspective shifts from modernist to postmodernist – thereafter solid modernist to liquid modernist – and in being robbed of an older particular, but inevitably singular, version of a Marxian critique, the reader of Bauman gains a new dysfunctional family of critical theory and the effect is far reaching as it offers some of his most telling contributions to sociology.

In this book I demonstrate how his shift in focus turned Bauman from a good sociologist into an international intellectual working in broad strokes that not only defy easy categorization but which also put him in the very first rank of sociologists of all time. My point is that really there is no comparison to be made between Bauman Mark One and Bauman Mark Two because the second is a different sociologist. The staples of his critical project may be the same, but Bauman Mark Two – the pre-eminent clocker of the *Zeitgeist* – understands that the world has changed in massively significant ways and it is the inescapability of this – as well as the fact that we have watched Bauman struggling for a half a century in a web of his own weaving – that makes his work matter. Bauman Mark Two emerged at a time when those outside sociology – in cultural studies in particular – were dismembering ideals which had prevailed since the Enlightenment, importing and concocting exotic techniques from postmodernism and poststructuralism – and he has come to be as commanding a representative of this phase in sociology as somebody like Richard Rorty is in philosophy.

Bauman is similar to Rorty in another key way too – he is not a thinker who will be remembered for his originality. But originality in any case is today a freighted quality, ironically bestowed and uneasily received, and true to form Bauman carries his own renown lightly. He does not have any pretensions towards it, because he knows that the best you can do in a world 'haunted by the excess of values worth pursuing' is give an impression of originality. And if this is an accurate assessment of Bauman's work, he gives a better impression than most. What he does do in his sociology is recover theories, ideas and concepts, rethink them and put them together to generate 'new' theories, ideas and concepts. In this sense, he is always adapting and expanding, acting not so much as an improver but as a poet given licence to turn what has become pedestrian into something fabulous.

The legacy of Bauman's influences is obvious right through his work, but he creates a sociological way of thinking that is very much his own. As I have argued elsewhere,[22] Bauman is the proselytizing sociologist *par excellence*, who, as a finder and re-assembler, has no equals and the result is that familiar ideas, theories and concepts announce themselves new-minted in his hands. As such his 'originality' lies in his ability to make connections which have not previously been articulated; he not only tells us what we can see, but what we cannot say; he also tells us things we do not know, cannot see. To this extent I argue that Bauman has transcended his influences – while he may not have created a sociology that his entirely his own, he has nonetheless concocted for us into one exotic dish a range of tantalizing flavours. And in writing this introductory book I am comforted by the fact that everywhere and always in his work, Bauman assigns his own meanings to these influences, to recreate them, as it were, into a definitive sociological hermeneutics that is very much his own.

PLACING THE MAN, PLACING HIS SOCIOLOGY

As V.S. Naipaul once said, every great writer is produced by a series of special circumstances. Born into a family of Jewish origin in Poznan, Poland in 1925, Bauman could be a character in a twentieth-century novel by the great Argentine writer, Jorge Luis Borges, an epic charting the peak and decline of the 'solid' *conjoncture* stage of modernity. As Keith Tester has pointed out, by the 'time he was twenty, Bauman had confronted anti-Semitism, Stalinism, Nazism and warfare'.[23] Despite fighting for his country against the Nazis during the Second World War 'Bauman was expelled from the army in 1953 during an anti-Semitic purge which was carried out in the name of the policy of the "de-Judaising of the army"'.[24] In 1968 Bauman was sacked from his Professorship at Warsaw University and expatriated from his country during another anti-Semitic purge. However, he did not become a global nomad like many other intellectuals exiled from the Eastern bloc – exiles everywhere and nowhere at home – because he found his second home in Leeds.

To this extent Bauman's biography is both like and unlike the stories of other modern men and women who came of age in Eastern Europe during the Second World War. His is a Polish-Jewish story that is both common and unlike others and there can be no doubting that his obsessions and interests have their genesis in his own individual biography. Indeed, Bauman's project is particularly fascinating for me not because it is 'sociological' or 'academic', but because his work is thoroughly self-absorbed and his autobiography intrudes throughout. As the reader will see, Bauman's interest in a number of themes, from consumer culture to community, to love and identity, resonate time and time again in his work, but not as much as the obvious axe he has to grind with modernity. Indeed, the point that Bauman's social identity is Jewish, Polish, British, socialist, professorial and the rest, means that the contingency of his subjectivity and extraneous historical circumstances is couched to be crucial in a particular way, which is unique to him, and which adds to our understanding of his work.

Bauman knows that by now it is nigh on impossible for sociologists to write anything new. I am of course being hypothetical here, but if he were asked why, I imagine that the acerbic sociologist would, in the manner of Borges, say that in his own particular case this is because he has lived for so long he has not only had most of the experiences that life has to offer but he has also already read everything of any use in social theory! Indeed, to read Bauman is to recognize that he is sociology's version of Denys the Alexandrian, who in Flaubert's account was the man who got orders from heaven to read every book in the world.[25] Bauman is the sociologist as reader, as definite and as marked a category as that of poet, for whom all the activity and pleasure of life derives from the experience of words. He loves books, he savours them, he devours them, and he wants to change the world with them. This is a man who takes such pleasure in reading that he is also able – seemingly effortlessly – to produce a most compelling critique of the world as it is in itself *erlebnis* for his own readers. Bauman's work is not simply sociology; it has the full force of the sociological imagination with it.[26]

My remarking that it is difficult for him to write anything new is not to suggest that as he greets his ninth decade Bauman's intellectual powers have diminished in the slightest. On the contrary, I want to stress that having the wisdom of an old man he has learned that it is impossible to write sociology without being influenced by what has already been written by other thinkers and to this extent Bauman recognizes both the conscious *and* the unconscious intertextuality that shapes his own work.

A large number of different thinkers have exerted their influences on Bauman and it would take another, different kind of book than this one to explain the implications of these. However, in making reference to Bauman's influences I should like to point out at the outset that there is no attempt here to contextualize his *oeuvre*, as grasping the enormity of this task would not only be too daunting a challenge for the introductory reader, but also too large an intellectual task for this author. It would be foolhardy anyway to attempt to give – in such a concise book as this at any rate – a voice and shape to an imagination that has spawned such a diverse project. However, in relation to ways in which Bauman's sociology has resonances with the work of other writers the reader will in the course of this introduction be able to identify two major groups of influences at the forefront of the discussion. It will quickly become apparent that Bauman tends to find fresh marrow even in the most well-picked bones of social theory and the major intertextual influences revealed in this book will be to a larger extent Richard Rorty, Jean Baudrillard, Jean-Paul Sartre and Sigmund Freud and to a lesser extent Michel Foucault, Antonio Gramsci and Agnes Heller. It will also become clear to the reader that not only does Bauman rely on social theorists to develop what is his own very specific kind of sociology, but that being a prolific reader of literature, he draws much of his inspiration from a wide range of novelists-cum-philosophers, but particularly Jorge Luis Borges, Italo Calvino and Milan Kundera.

The ideas and standpoints of another disparate group of social theorists also loom large in this book. Since I agree with Peter Beilharz that Bauman is the world's 'greatest living sociologist' and believe that it is his work that sets the standards by which all others should be measured – quite simply there is nobody else like him in sociology today – I constantly draw on the work of other key figures in social theory, most of whom are his contemporaries, as a critical backcloth to both develop and demonstrate the explanatory power of Bauman's own sociology.

DEALING WITH BAUMAN'S SINGULARITY

Taking Bauman's sociology as a totality – as we must if we are to gain a proper understanding of its ways and means – does not mean that everything in it is seamless or that there are inconsistencies, nor does the fact that Bauman writes prolifically mean that his sociology lacks a centre. Rather it signals a deeper sense that there are many ways in which the sociologist can develop his understanding of the world. Most sociologists follow a particular school of thought and/or stick to what they know best. In Bauman's case, the cumulative effect gets more compelling the more he writes, the more directions he goes in, the more powerful his sociology convinces. This is because Bauman is still interested in surprising himself.

Another of Bauman's greatest gifts is his ability to recognize the difference between sociology as it as become domesticated by academic careerism and the demands of the RAE[27] – pointless and inevitable – and sociology that is alert to life as it is lived: relentless, unpredictable, ambivalent. In common with existentialists such as Sartre, Bauman not only understands that the world is human but also that the human 'being-in-the-world' is only understandable through a critical engagement with it. As the reader will see, Bauman doesn't so much transport his readers to another place, so much as awaken their consciousnesses or sociological imaginations to the already existing reality in which they find themselves and all that that implies.

As Bauman points out, today we live in a sociality of individuals who think of themselves at centre stage and growing ever more palpable – figures at the hub of the present. Accordingly a sociology geared to understanding the conditions of the world as one of relentless change needs 'to replace the category of *society* with that of *sociality*; a category that tries to convey the processual modality of social reality, the dialectical play of randomness and pattern (or, from the agent's point of view, of freedom and dependence); and a category that refuses to take the structured character of the process for granted – which treats instead all found structures as emergent accomplishments'.[28] Bauman is concerned more than any other thinker today with this kind of insistency that is the central feature of contemporary life and the prickly particularity of individual lives, especially the enduring problem of how individual men and women deal with others apparently just as crippled by anxiety, risk and uncertainty as they are themselves.

As I have suggested already, Bauman's sociology employs a breadth of erudition that takes the reader across and down layers of accrued meanings, not to mention the specialized jargons and lexicons of sociology and social philosophy. That his work is informed by a vast amount of reading, and its range and pitch, are concomitantly daunting for the uninitiated. The task of writing an introduction to Bauman's sociological approach is also made more difficult by virtue of the fact that it is nigh on impossible to pin his sociology down, which makes it difficult to outline and explain the bare bones of his sociological approach in the usual introductory fashion. Bauman's sociology is not dependent in a single style, manner or theoretical framework. He has no taste for schools of thought, for maintaining schools or trends. In marked contrast to some sociologists, Bauman knows that there is nothing to be gained from imposing rigid theoretical frameworks or interpretations on patterns of behaviour where none exist. While others are busy identifying themselves in the popular esteem of the ideas of the 'Founding Fathers', Bauman's recital of their views and achievements is much less deferent and he only draws on them if they offer him the opportunity to recognize some present violations of freedom, of responsibility.

Consequently Bauman's sociology does not in any way or form represent a particular school of thought, as in Norbert Elias's figuration-alism, for example.[29] On the contrary, his sociology is full of arbitrary riches rather than engineered instruction – there are no lesson plans in the pages or in their arrangement. Bauman's books enable the reader to read dispositionally rather than methodically – he does not offer a toolkit in the way that say Pierre Bourdieu does[30] – and you build rather a sense of his current interests, the habits of his mind, and the associative trails these take, the fragments, the jolts, new beginnings and the revisitings, in each new piece of work.

It needs to be grasped from the outset that the aim of Bauman's sociology is not to reconstruct 'the classical foundation texts of sociology as building blocks for his own comprehensive social theory' in the manner of Habermas[31] or provide it with some 'new rules of sociological method' *vis-à-vis* Anthony Giddens.[32] Instead, Bauman merely wants to better reconcile sociology with the way in which the already existing reality actually is, but in a way that, if it needs to be 'a theory of contemporary society', is always imbued with the warmth of human life, a warmth that would fade from sociology were it to follow the intellectual trajectories suggested by Habermas and Giddens. Bauman's sociology always has the force of life in it and to read him is to see that he is forever and always concerned with the ways in which people live today, but more than that, even, he is concerned with everyday human concerns to do with community, of love and memory and the pain and happiness they bring, the way that people exist in their own minds and the minds of others. For Bauman, being-for-others is the only authentic way a sociologist can work, can live his life. This is why he believes it is its close attention to humankind's responsibility for the other that should give sociology its thumping heart.

Quite simply, there is nobody else like him in sociology today. He is a sociologist who has his own, complete, individuality. He runs alone; he is a loner by temperament and has no particular sociological affiliations. He belongs to no sociological school of thought and he ploughs a lone furrow. The great strength of Bauman's way of thinking sociologically is in his keen existential insight and his refusal to think inside the usual sociology box, as well as his ability to analyse and speculate about what it means to live in the contemporary world without stooping to any easy conclusions. To this end he has created his own particular style *and* substance for doing sociology, which is unique to him and although the muscle of Bauman's work is its sociological detail, its strength comes from its commingling of a rigorous analysis with a highly perceptive sociological imagination.

BAUMAN AND BAUDRILLARD

The above points notwithstanding, Bauman creates in his sociology a scenic train ride which nonetheless retains many of the features of the founding fathers – at its centre there beats the heart of a nineteenth-century classic. But instead of looking for orthodox claims to truth in certainist theories and concepts, he offers something else: a style of sociology that has many affinities with the radical innovations of the postmodernist Jean Baudrillard. There are major differences, though. Bauman may flirt with parody and irony but he does not succumb to their seductions. He never retreats into the nihilism of postmodernism. Contrary to post-modernism, in Bauman's sociology the already existing reality might be pregnant with possibility but it is as solidly material as Marx always said it was. In this way, his sociology provides a corrective to the nihilism found in the work of Baudrillard, which if it trims down the everyday to a series of fast-flowing images, simultaneously reduces sociology to the equivalent of watching TV. As Bauman puts it:

> Personal experiences can be enclosed by the frame of the television screen. One doubts whether the world can. One suspects, *pace* Baudrillard, that there is life left after and beyond the television. To many people, much in their life is anything but simulation. To many, reality remains what it always used to be: tough, solid, resistant and harsh. They need to sink their teeth into some quite real bread before they abandon themselves to munching images.[33]

Watching the everyday can seem irksome – like watching somebody else's home videos over and again – which relates to what people do that is structured and structuring about their everyday lives. That is those experiences which are not an unfolding reality but are the habitual and routine actions and behaviours that are in some sense 'ready-made', as if taken out of a drawer and set to work. But, for Bauman, the real does not have to be understood as a representation, but those myriad spaces where the already existing reality of the world unfolds in all its quotidian simplicity. Bauman deconstructs the dichotomy between 'realist' and 'idealist' truth claims about whether there is or is not a 'real' world at the drop of a hat by making the simple assumption that there is something like the 'real' world, something like an 'actually existing reality'. In this sense, the challenge Bauman sets himself in his sociology is to reach the world and make it intelligible for his audience rather than to find some truth.

Unlike Baudrillard's work, Bauman's sociology is more than a style; it is governed by a substance, too. Baudrillard's sociology is a fantasy work that is written in a way that parodies the conventions of sociology by plunging us toward the base and baseness of a hyperreal post-social society, but using the quotidian as a sort of theme park cannot say anything authoritative about anything in terms fitting to the 'real' world. Bauman would not go as far as Baudrillard and suggest that modernity has been transformed *ad infinitum* into a cultural desert where everything to do with life that is genuine or authentic has been closed down and replaced with an artificial, or at the best, virtual existence. In marked contrast to Baudrillard, Bauman can see ways of escape from this insulated hyperreality, but as we shall see he is sceptical as to whether or not people have the necessary desire to make the leap of faith required. But on another level Bauman is indebted to Baudrillard, because it was he who helped to liberate his sociological imagination in the same way that Bauman himself has liberated others.

The reader will see that Bauman's sociology maintains a steadfast, somewhat traditional sense of what sociology is, should be. To this extent he is on the face of it a classical sociologist in whose work elements of the radicalism of poststructuralism and postmodernism are temperately permitted to emerge. Yet because his intellectual curiosity with the themes and ideas he has learned from Baudrillard compel him to disrupt the sociological orthodoxy he is so anxious to preserve, there is always a tension in his work. Bauman therefore remains that ambivalent rarity, a critic of sociology who clings on to his Enlightenment faith in sociology to change the world for the better, for humanity.

BAUMAN AND FOUCAULT

The last point notwithstanding, Bauman's understanding of sociological knowledge is also opposite to the Enlightenment ideal. For Bauman, as for Foucault, knowledge is cultural rather than universal and it is contingent rather than cumulative. This is not only because Bauman's sociology recognizes that culture is praxis, but also because, like Foucault, he is sceptical about what science can tell us about humankind and his *oeuvre* operates in that 'critical shuttle between consciousness and unconsciousness'.[34] However, where Bauman parts company with Foucault is in his understanding of the benefits of phenomenology for the sociological enterprise. Whereas Foucault is intent on purging knowledge of the 'anthropologism' that blights phenomenological analysis and replacing it with an 'archaeology' which has as its critical thrust a method of structural linguistics for uncovering pre-existing 'subject' positions in systems of discourse, Bauman maintains that the goal of sociological analysis must always be the already existing human world *Erlebnis*.

For a long time – even before the emergence of poststructuralism – ethnographers and other qualitative-minded sociologists have been grappling with the difficulty of the twin tasks of on the one hand identifying through their methodologies the experiences of human consciousness and unconsciousness and on the other conveying these on the written page. In the pages of his books, Bauman certainly has a good try at it by situating human subjectivity in the context of a generalist sociology. It is not often that sociologists demonstrate the confidence or the ability to project onto the pages of their books the private worlds of individuals, their dreams – what goes on inside their heads – but that is what the reader gets from Bauman. In the course of offering this counter position he does not so much retreat into the kind of phenomenology rejected by Foucault and other poststructuralists, but instead offers an alternative way of painting the world, altering the concept of what we understand as the 'real' of the already existing reality in the process.

With Bauman, readers will find that the quotidian is not reduced to interaction between pre-existing 'subject' positions in systems of discourse in the Foucauldian manner. On the contrary, they will find that it is with 'things as they are' in the Kantian meaning that Bauman's sociology is concerned, because it is the already existing reality, the world as it appears to individuals themselves in the quotidian, that matters to ordinary men and women. For Bauman, the everyday is where life is lived, immersed in the ordinary, and sociology is the means which reveals it to be extraordinary.

Bauman's aim is to reconcile sociology with the way the already existing reality actually is. The irony is, of course, that his ways and means of achieving this have been accused by his critics of lacking a sense of realism, because he does not develop an empirical approach which deals with primary research methodologies: the narrow kind of empirical sociology which tends to switch between individuating and totalizing descriptions of the world 'out there', and in the process making them equivalent in specificity to the imagined reality being addressed. In some of his less engaged readers there is a wish for some primary empirical detail to support the arguments, but as I demonstrate in the following pages, that is to misunderstand Bauman's project. In marked contrast to his critics, Bauman recognizes in his sociology contingency that unbridgeable gap between what sociologists say about the world and what may actually be going on in the world. Moreover, sociologists like Bauman work at an intuitive level that does not require them to explain why they have done something 'this way' rather than another.

Yet Bauman's is a deeply humanist project that leaves its readers thinking about life's endless complexities and the day-to-day dilemmas it continues to pose and to this extent it restores a humanized view of the already existing reality to social theory. But if it is not the naive cosy or homely view of 'things as they are' which is so derided by the poststructuralists, it is a kind of sociology which insists that human faces come before everything else. As Bauman points out in *Postmodern Ethics*,[35] faces are the first we see of each other. In looking into the face of the other we are reminded that we are engaged in a human encounter, person to person, that comes with the face. In refusing to efface the face from social analysis, what Bauman presents us with is a humanistic sociology which is not only able to capture the surface experiences of human life, but is also capable of uncovering a sense of those lives lived from within, which many other interpreters regularly claim to see, but in their analyses hardly ever reach.

BAUMAN AND THE CONTINUING RELEVANCE OF SOCIOLOGY

I should like to stress at the outset that the point of this introduction is not to imprison Bauman in a definitive box; it is an attempt to expand the grasp of his sociology to those who are not familiar with and/or are apprehensive of his work. Like most other projected studies, this one underwent a number of sea changes until it eventually became this book. At first, I tried to incorporate into the discussion his entire book-length published work, but as the project developed it became more and more evident that a great deal of what is significant about Bauman was slipping through the net. I considered that if what was left was all-encompassing it neither adequately reflected Bauman's key ideas nor did it make these any more palatable to an introductory audience. My own choice of topics has for the most part been determined not so much by Bauman's interests but because the central bases of his thought can be most 'perspicuously articulated'[36] through them. With this in mind I gradually began to shift the emphasis until it dawned on me that Bauman ought to be read with the eyes firmly planted on the audience for sociology. Bauman recognizes that we today live in a new era – what in his writings he calls liquid modernity – and sociology is addressing a new audience.

This introduction aims to provide a more straightforward context for a greater appreciation and understanding of a sociologist whose work is not only defined by our times, but also defines our times. The choice of emphasis adopted in the book then is based on Bauman's argument that the audience of sociology is changing and that accordingly sociology must change if it is to continue having a critical resonance. As Bauman points out, sociology today operates less and less as a fulcrum between itself and integrated, organized and administered institutions, such as the state, in the acknowledged *legislating* manner of yesteryear, but more and more in an unacknowledged *interpreting* manner which, if not always instantly recognizable to its new decentred public, is nonetheless embodied with a dialectic which, to use Anthony Giddens's apt expression, is reflective of the double hermeneutic[37] that is the measure of the social world as it is constituted on the one hand by sociologists and on the other by 'lay actors'.

The lesson at the heart of Bauman's project is that the accounts of the already existing reality we get from the sociology textbooks are too often domesticated versions of the real thing. Bauman recognizes too that sociology only lives as long as sociologists can make use of its concepts. As he has suggested, the language of sociology is still too often 'nineteenth-centuryish'[38] and it does not yet have an appropriate lexicon through which it can grapple with the twinned fortunes of freedom and security, the past and the present. To put it another way, the world of the present is another country where people do things differently from the past and we may well ask whether sociology is still abroad when its protagonists attempt to 'fully grasp its mechanism and momentum'.[39] As has been intimated already, Bauman knows that the quotidian is not only more unpredictable but for this very reason is more difficult to classify than some sociologists would have it. In marked contrast to these sociologists, Bauman knows that there is nothing to be gained from imposing rigid theoretical frameworks or interpretations on patterns of behaviour where none exist. And he isn't going to portray for us solid figures with vices and virtues painted upon them in the legislating manner of nineteenth-century sociology. For Bauman, culture is praxis and far from acting as a mere prerequisite of 'normative integration' in the structural functionalist sense, culture gives individuals a sense of the world beyond their own, providing them with access to the dialectic between the self and Other, the familiar and the unfamiliar.[40]

Bauman is going to chart for us instead the trajectories of lives made real by the contingency and ambivalence events. Bauman recognizes that today most of us live in-between lives – between classes, between cultures, between communities – in which we jump like a switchback ride in a world where no one seems quite to know what is going on, and just about anything seems possible. Bauman's sociology recognizes that if the world we inhabit has shifted from a more structured *society* to a decentred *sociality* in which individuality dominates more than anything else, it is also a world which encourages separation, valorizes solitude and aloneness, and removes individuals from the anchors that initially formed them.

While classical Marxism was uninterested in individuals, preferring instead to think of the individual as an upshot of consistent, collective and interdependent roles, Bauman is delighted to put them at the forefront of his analyses. He recognizes that people have increasingly come to expect that personal relations – rather than social class, community or kindred relationships – are the sole means of self-expression and self-actualization.

In this sense, Bauman's sociology is a critical account of human individuality and the irrepressibility of men and women in their busy pursuit of individual happiness. He recognizes that a key ingredient of this new individuality is a self that if it is characterized by supreme selfishness is also likely to be something insubstantial, inchoate and fragmented. Indeed, the sense of being constantly in motion is what underpins life today and as Bauman puts it, to 'be of any use to its new potential audience, sociology needs to offer knowledge that chimes with their experience and corresponds to their problems and tasks'.[41]

Reading Bauman is like finding out that someone has finally started building a new stretch of motorway running from the remnants of orthodox sociology after its drawn out but hesitant dabble with postmodernism. And what the reader will see in the following chapters is that in developing a new direction for sociology Bauman has not exactly reinvented the wheel, but he has given it a new tread, and even more importantly, he's made sure that it is still roadworthy. The reason why Bauman is so important is the dawning realization in sociology and beyond that he belongs to an extraordinary moment in sociological thought when there is a shared belief that after poststructuralism and postmodernism a new beginning, or at the very least a realignment of sociology, is necessary. This author believes that those who want to understand that moment and take its challenges seriously must read Bauman. This is because his sociology more than any other currently on offer chimes with the lives and times of the contemporary world we inhabit. And as I demonstrate in the following pages this challenge not only strikes at the heart of sociology but also reverberates across other disciplines such as cultural studies, tourism studies, criminology, human geography, social philosophy, social policy and many more, contesting their received notions and opening up new ways of thinking about the world in the process.

2

Bauman's Sociology: His Theory of Modernity

> Theories differ not by their appetite for selection, but by what they
> select. Selection as such they cannot (and shall not, if they wish to
> be of use) avoid; the point is to make the right selection, or rather
> a better selection than the one the theory intends to improve on,
> complement or replace. That is, to focus the searchlights and the
> spotlights in a way that would assist orientation and help to find
> the way; on paths and crossroads, but also on bogs and landmines
> …

Zygmunt Bauman[1]

As that most perceptive of 20th-century philosophers, Michel Foucault,
once observed, how any thinker – including, though not exclusively,
sociologists – classifies and explains away social phenomena tells readers
more about the thinker, about his or her 'stance on how things are, than it
does about any truth … It tells more about that which is true to the namer'.[2]
Indeed, if there is one thing that all the books in the *Key Sociologists*
series have in common, and what they each reveal in their pages, is that
every single one of the sociologists they deal with has a story that is
constant, a story they each tell, a story they develop their ideas around,

and keep on repeating, consciously or not. The most original of the *Key Sociologists* have their own stories, while some of them rely on someone else's story to develop their own ideas. Then there are those who, I should like to argue, are the truly great sociologists. These are the *Key Sociologists* who, in the formative years of their academic careers, rely on the stories of others, but who reach a point when they recognize the story they have been repeating has run out of disguises, and what they do is set about starting over again, but this time they want to make their own way of seeing the world rather than rely on someone else's vision. It is perhaps fitting that the career of Zygmunt Bauman should have the mark of such ambivalence: a sociologist whose earliest work, in common with many of his contemporaries, followed a well-beaten path, but who was destined to become himself the real thing – the greatest original thinking sociologist of the contemporary era.

BAUMAN MARK ONE

Like most other leftist sociologists writing during the 1960s, 1970s and early 1980s, the story that Bauman Mark One worked with was Marxism.[3] This was not unusual by any means since, as Foucault has remarked, at this time 'there was a certain way of thinking correctly, a certain style of political discourse, a certain ethics of the intellectual. One *had* to be on familiar terms with Marx'.[4] Frank Parkin confirmed Foucault's claim when he wrote the revised edition of his *Max Weber*[5] in the *Key Sociologists* series in 2002. As he put it, when the book was originally published twenty years previously it 'was a time when Marxist theory … ruled the intellectual roost, not only by defining the terms of debate but also by turning out an endless supply of conceptual tools with which to conduct it. Almost every corner of the social sciences and beyond came to absorb the language of the Marxist renaissance', or so it seemed.

As every first-year undergraduate sociology student who leaves university for the summer recess is aware, the story that Marxists work with assumes that people's motivations, values and beliefs are derivative of their social class position and their material interests. In a nutshell, the material economic base determines the superstructure of society's institutions, and society itself is characterized by a class struggle arising from the means of production. These students also know that Marxism's great theme in all its versions is one about the possibility of 'man' overcoming his four-fold alienation – from himself, from his fellow-man, from his work and his products – and gaining his freedom through equality in a future communist society which will once and for all put an end to 'pre-history' and allow 'real history' to begin.[6] By the 1980s, however, Bauman, in common with many other leftist thinkers, was no longer persuaded by this story, it no longer worked for him the way it had done previously.

As the reader will recall, in the first chapter of this book I suggested that the major thrust of the critical turn in Bauman's work came with the publication of *Legislators and Interpreters* in 1987. According to Bauman, the legislators are those intellectuals who make authoritative ideological statements about the world and who have the power to make the '*procedural rules* which assure the attainment of truth, the arrival of moral judgement, and the selection of proper artistic taste. Such procedural rules have a *universal validity*, as to the *products* of their application'.[7] Without oversimplifying the thrust of my argument, I want to suggest that by the 1980s Bauman had come to recognize that in attempting to revise orthodox Marxism he was merely conspiring to defend its legislating 'perfection'; and as a result his own ideas had to remain secondary and subservient to the metaphysical structure that he had inherited from Marx.

BAUMAN MARK TWO

Bauman Mark Two came into being at a time when those outside sociology – in fields as diverse as architecture and philosophy – were dismembering ideals which had prevailed since the Enlightenment, importing and concocting new and outlandish techniques, which some people were now calling postmodernism – and he emerged as a commanding representative of this phase in sociology as Charles Jencks was in architecture, Hayden White was in historiography and as Richard Rorty was in philosophy. Indeed, from the publication of *Legislators and Interpreters* onwards there is a move in Bauman's sociology which has the effect of a parallax; the perspective shifts from modernist to postmodernist – thereafter solid modernist to liquid modernist – and in being robbed of an older particular, but inevitably singular version of a Marxist critique, the reader of Bauman gains a new dysfunctional family of critical theory and the effect is far reaching as it offers some of his most telling contributions to sociology.

The sociology of Bauman Mark Two did not suddenly explode, but smouldered for some time before bursting into flame. If much of Bauman's writing in the late 1980s was spent coming to terms with the postmodern turn and the implications of this for developing his approach to sociology, the 1990s saw him mapping out a thoroughgoing critique of modernity. He was now on a quest for his own vision and his exploded imagination needed a larger canvas than the Marxist focus on social class, and it was the idea of modernity that increasingly came to both compel and exasperate him. However, before we consider Bauman's ambivalent fascination with modernity, it is first of all important to discuss the major reasons why he came to feel increasingly alienated from Marxism.

THE BREAK WITH MARXISM

The first reason why Bauman felt let down by Marxism was that it relied too heavily on out-dated and reified or abstract concepts. The problem for Marxism was that by the 'postmodern' turn in social theory in the 1980s it was increasingly looking like a parody of itself: a critical perspective built on the concepts that merely mimicked the classifying habits of the modernist sensibility that other more poststructuralist and postmodernist inclined commentators were hell bent on deconstructing. But perhaps more worryingly, the concepts Marxism had traditionally worked with – 'social class', 'alienation', 'ideology' and the rest – no longer seemed to have any practical content. It was becoming more and more difficult to relate them to concrete social relations, particularly in light of the accelerated social and cultural change that had emerged with the 'long sixties'.[8]

As Bauman makes clear in *Memories of Class*, the problem with Marxism was that it failed to provide an adequate account of the monumental changes in modern industrial capitalism which had seen consumption and consumer culture taking the place of production and work.[9] In a nutshell, the world had changed but orthodox Marxism was still working on the assumption that the problems of injustice and inequality could be identified with social class relations. Not only this, but there was a powerful singularity of vision in the Marxist view of the world that meant that it was also still operating with a reified conception of social class characterized by the image of a particular *habitus* which assumed that the basic securities and affiliations of custom, community and familial relations, which had been established with the emergence of modern industrial capitalism, for the most part still prevailed. And the irony was that if people were no longer living daily with the knowledge of a 'tightly structured time-space and the solidity and durability of the world',[10] Marxism seemed to be offering the view that if life for 'the working class' was still unjust it was also pretty much unchanging and predictable.[11]

What Marxism could not grasp in effect was the sense of a discontinuity in the course of the *longue durée* of modernity. Modernity was not only becoming more disorganized and uncertain – particularly with the collapse of its industrial base – but it was also in the process of erasing many of the established traces of the social class *habitus* Marxism had taken for granted and what it had heretofore tacitly associated with organized industrial labour. As Keith Tester[12] points out, Bauman identified three features relating to this shifting world which challenged the orthodox Marxist view of social class:

> First, he pointed out that the working class of large-scale industrial production was contracting on an annual basis. Second, the working class had morally and spatially fractured, its old concentrations dissipated: 'Gone or almost gone is that working class *moral destiny*, which came together with *physical destiny*. New workers are sprinkled amidst faceless residential estates whose inhabitants are united by the way they spend their money, not the way they earn it'[13] ... Third, the nature of work had changed: 'Most of the new generation of workers are occasional, temporary and part-time. They neither can nor wish to think of their jobs as a life-long occupation ... They come and go, much as those people whom they meet on the way'.[14]

What Bauman was suggesting was that it no longer made any sense to reduce social class to relations between industrial capital and wage-labour. But orthodox Marxism was oblivious to this because it emphasized in its manifestos similarity rather than difference, fixity rather than contingency: incongruities that were now constantly being undermined and disrupted in a world that had become stubbornly insistent on change. As Bauman saw it, he no longer had the same part and a purpose for orthodox Marxism in his schema because it assumed that the majority lived 'working class' lives huddled together through an intimacy that left them essentially untouched, waiting for some never-to-be-realized worker's paradise which would never arrive. The Marxist bubble had burst and its trademark brand of still trying to fit 'the working class' into a prefabricated template in order to fit the thematic of the never-to-be-realized worker's paradise simply did not work any more.

As Bauman points out, for all the conceptual sophistication Marxism had gained during the 1960s and 1970s, it was still thoroughly '"economistic", and in most cases severely reductionist'.[15] It worked with the assumption that the working class lived largely stable lives straitened by unknowingness and deference and which were not yet threatened by consumer novelties. It assumed working class lives involved singular ways of living and were bound by iron rules about where they could go and what they could do – the working classes appearing increasingly in its analyses like zombie characters of a world that was no more. Marxism still assumed that working class lives depended on single questions with enduring solutions: where would they work? who would they marry? It still largely assumed that by and large most people were stuck in the social class into which they were born. But as Bauman points out, if in solid modernity identity was one accepting sameness and a very limited range of difference, in liquid modernity it had become for the majority a matter of asserting their individuality and not only accepting but trying to cope with a life of seemingly inbuilt inexorable change. As a result the enforced normalization of any one way of life was increasingly being rejected. Contrary to Marxism, people were more and more confronted with lives that had become more rich and complex.

For Bauman, the reasons why people were rejecting lives made to the measure of social class were plain to see; they restricted other potential outlets for credulity – they only gave people so many varieties of identity they could choose from. In his sociology written in the 1980s, Bauman was acutely aware that since the period of the long sixties solid modern lives, hemmed in by moral forces and social restrictions about 'knowing your place', and as a result placing conformity over revolt, duty over self-fulfilment, were increasingly being rejected. What Marxist commentators could not get their heads around was that modernity had turned itself into a gleeful dismantling of an orderly life – as Bauman puts it, drawing on Giddens's phraseology – one of perpetual disembedding and re-embedding. If in solid modernity the questions of 'who am I?' and 'what am I to be?' became increasingly a matter of individual choice and individual commitment, as opposed to an obligation and commitment imposed on the community (and by that what is meant is 'imposed on the community' not 'imposed on individuals by the community'; the individual did not exist in the modern sense), with the emergence of liquid modernity they began to take on unprecedented (individual) conviction. And accordingly modern lives had become more than ever before the fruit of contingency: of existential subjectivity and chance associations and a life involving constantly stripping away what was formerly assumed to be locked in place.

Marxism and consumer culture

When Marx remarked in *Capital*[16] that 'money and commodity cannot take themselves to the market; they cannot exchange themselves', he was not only demonstrating his attentiveness to the centrality that commodity fetishism would come to play in the perpetuation of the capitalist mode of production, but also to the ambivalence of consumption facing every capitalist: that when workers become consumers their specificity as workers is eclipsed. And he 'saw here the great illusion of every capitalist who wished only that other workers, not his own, confront him as consumers'.[17] Yet despite Marx's own shrewd grasp of consumer culture, by the 1980s the majority of orthodox Marxist accounts were still ignoring the changed climatic conditions of advanced capitalism and following their mentor; they were still offering analyses which were at once 'productionist', 'workerist' and 'masculinist'. As a result, in their analyses, they were neither able to re-imagine 'workers' recast as 'consumers' – they merely saw workers consuming – who were increasingly able to occupy the place of consumption, nor to anticipate the implications of the development of the commodity relation on a global scale.

Bauman saw that what was needed was a sociology that recognized that many of the concepts that used to sustain it had dissolved in the explosion of individualism and materialism, particularly since the 1960s. Bauman argued that individual choice much more than social class or any other kind of social stratification was now regulating populations and hedging personal inclinations. Contrary to Marxism, Bauman's work was suggesting that when you are supposed to know your place in the world, there is no imaginative pleasure greater then slipping your moorings. Being liquid modern – as opposed to solid modern – means living and believing in ways *other* than those made tacit by one's own group's version of the already existing reality. What Bauman was suggesting in his work, particularly from the publication of *Freedom* onwards, was that modern living had become not so much a work of the imagination as a DIY themed thrill ride, which meant that people had become perfectly contented to exploit other authorized ways of being in the world. And just as the mines and the steelworks of yore had formed the industrial working class, the glitteringly enticing shopping mall was increasingly forming the consumerist masses into what was in effect a new stage of modernity.

What Bauman saw was a world that was saying to individuals: forget who you are and if you cannot be what you want to be, imagine that you can. Marxism had failed to recognize that modernity had transformed itself into a world where people, no matter what their status at birth, were increasingly refusing to accept the way they were supposed to live, recognizing as they did that their lives were now about choice, not about situation. If, for Walter Benjamin,[18] in his *Arcades Project*, consumers began to think of themselves as a mass, it was with the establishment of post-Fordist production that they were able to re-think of themselves as individualized consumers. It is a simple point that Bauman perhaps does not make explicitly enough, but liquid modernity emerged at a time when the majority of people – for the first time – could afford to consume items that were not necessary for survival or necessity.

Bauman certainly wasn't the first social theorist to rethink social class relationships in this way. Some cultural Marxist theorists, most particularly those associated with the Frankfurt School,[19] had since the Second World War been developing a more sophisticated form of critical theory which suggested that it is not impossible to separate human consciousness from the material existence of people's lived condition. And in so doing they had offered an alternative Marxist theory of the modern world, which suggested that everything the masses see is mediated through the filter of the 'culture industry'. As is well known, Adorno and Horkheimer[20] asserted that men and women may think that they are free, but they are only free 'to choose an ideology – since ideology always reflects economic coercion – everywhere proves to be freedom to choose what is always the same'. But if, for Adorno and Horkheimer, it was 'monopoly' and 'sameness' that were the two important defining features of the 'culture industry' which related to individuals in their role as consumers, Bauman was alerting us to the crucial point that in liquid modernity it is 'polysemy' and 'difference'. More than even those early critics of consumer culture could ever imagine, Bauman was suggesting that the denizens of liquid modernity stagger under the weight of an accumulation of consumer culture which is thoroughly 'individualized' in order to cater for differentiation.

The changing face of ideology

As the reader will see in Chapter 4, Bauman's concern with intellectuals and the cultural features of social relations is what links his work to the cultural Marxism of Antonio Gramsci. However, the Gramscian idea of hegemony is not a central concept in Bauman's sociology, not least because he recognizes that the legitimations of solid modernity which were based on hegemonic pathways are no longer ideologically powerful enough to hold sway in liquid modernity.[21] With the benefit of having read Foucault in the 1980s, Bauman was able to recognize the significance of the decentred power-knowledge of the ideologies (or discursive formations in Foucault's lexicon) which, with their consumer truth claims, allow their protagonists to evaporate from view at the same time as they blend into other hegemonic equivalences. However, whereas even the most sophisticated of Marxist commentators always sees the worm of ideology in every apple and with it the consequences which reduce its victims to a kind of *action without knowledge* – otherwise read as 'false consciousness', Bauman offers a critical theory which understands the relationship between the decentred oppressors who pull the invisible strings of their 'happy' victims as one of exploitation which is contingent through and through. And as he asserts in *Intimations of Postmodernity*, liquid modernity is 'modernity emancipated from false consciousness'.[22] In this sense, Bauman, recognizes that capitalism wants nothing from consumers but their capacity 'to stay in the game and have enough tokens left on the table to go on playing',[23] but he also understands, in common with Žižek,[24] that the contingent worlds that constitute liquid modernity operate as a matter of *action in spite of knowledge*; individuals in their liquid modern roles as consumers are not so much brainwashed as lacking the appetite for the class struggle – beliefs and ideologies are relegated to the background, while a hegemonic embracement of capitalism discloses a sense of what is at stake in the war against ambivalence.

In this sense, Bauman's sociology captures the irony that if for the majority of men and women solid modernity was a time when freedom was seen as an astonishing but largely unachievable hope, in the time of liquid modernity they appear to be prepared to surrender their hard-fought freedoms to the vast decentred power-knowledge of consumer capitalism which they happily allow to not so much regulate, as deregulate their lives. To put it another way, rather than just being a 'January' or 'Summer' treat, the 'sales' have become a ubiquitous feature of the liquid modern landscape and Bauman recasts men and women as ubiquitous sale shoppers too heavily weighed down by all the delightful purchases they have been making to devote any of their time to more serious issues. And regardless of their knowledgeability, liquid modern men and women are even prepared to embrace the burgeoning debt culture that accompanies this shop-until-you-drop performance.

In the event, Marxists and other more contemporary adherents of ideological explanations, such as Habermas, are confronted with the quandary of revealing 'structures of domination when no one is dominating, nothing is being dominated, and no ground exists for a principle of liberation from domination'.[25] As Bauman suggests, it is the configuration of economic arrangements associated with consumer capitalism which is of far greater importance for explaining patterns of social control today. To put it another way, social control like much else in liberal democracies has by and large been commodified and privatized. The comfortable majority no longer live in the shadow of tyranny of the state; instead they create their own turmoil, or in Baudrillard's terminology, their own paroxysm,[26] driven by market forces that they have no authority over, but at the same time have no final authority over them. The turmoil is barely noticeable – publicly at least – it is simply how people live. As Bauman puts it, it's as if 'we have been trained to stop worrying about things which stay stubbornly beyond our power ... and to concentrate our attention and energy instead on the tasks within our (individual) reach, competence and capacity for consumption.[27]

In liquid modernity, private consumption replaces work as the backbone of the reward system in a sociality which is underpatterned rather than patterned, disorganized rather than ordered. It is only the poor – the 'flawed consumers'[28] – who are still controlled through the work ethic. To put it simply, liquid modernity redraws the boundaries between social class divisions as a relationship between those who happily consume and those who cannot, despite their want of trying. Instead of being repressively controlled, this fragmented sociality is driven by the 'pleasure principle'. Social control is barely noticeable, except for the flawed consumers, whose subordinate position prevents them from participating freely in what has become for the masses a dream world of consumption. Bauman implies that what we are dealing with in liquid modernity is the kind of sociality, described by Albert Camus in the opening chapter of his book *The Rebel*, that is knowledgeable but is incapable of contemplating itself, and which asks no questions because it allows consumer culture to provide all the answers – in other words a sociality which has not learned rebellion.

Accordingly Bauman suggests that we need to recognize that it is not ideology but the power of seduction that is central to understanding the social control of the majority in liquid modernity.[29] As Kilminster and Varcoe[30] point out, if there is one recurring theme in Bauman's sociology, it is power – an approach to power relations, however, that allows him to move his analysis beyond the narrow confines of ideology and social class inequalities and which understands the various but changing divisions of interest found in the decentred sociality that is liquid modernity. Particularly in his writings after the 1980s, Bauman realized that sociologists were dealing with a society that had changed but which presented them with something particularly difficult to understand: reflexive human beings who are very individualistic, but at the same time need something to which they can belong. He also recognized in his sociology that if people do not spend much time analysing the world in which they live, they readily intuit it and embody it in the surface appearance of their identities.

As Bauman suggests in both *Freedom* and *Intimations of Post-modernity*, it is the willingness to be seduced – but not in any deep way – combined with something to believe in and belong to, that drives liquid modern men and women. Indeed, it is faith – whatever its ephemeral currency – rather than ideological control that is key to understanding the ways and means that seduction works in the lives of ordinary men and women: faith in the clothes they buy, their faith in themselves, their faith in their relationships, their faith in the market, their faith in religion – faith is all the rage. As Baudrillard has put it in another context, today we live in a world governed not by ideology but by the cult of 'the into'.[31] Yet Bauman is at pains to point out that for all its surface toughness and apparent impregnability, we should remember that faith is a surprisingly fragile thing, liable to shatter if its adherents lose the slightest bit of interest.

Marxism as a modern legislating theory

> No single-factor model is likely ever to account for the complexity of 'lived world' and embrace the totality of human experience. This general rule also applied to the truncated, shrunk and dessicated version of Marxism.
>
> Zygmunt Bauman[32]

Bauman was also now in a position to reread orthodox Marxism as a modern totalizing systematic theory which was underpinned by a naïve deterministic dialectical materialism that led its key proponents down the road of believing they could explain and unify everything. By the 1980s, Bauman recognized that he had not only run out of disguises for orthodox Marxism, but that he had to abandon it because it was the only way that he could move his own ideas forward. In this respect Bauman was by now arguing that the role of sociologists is to interpret rather than to legislate.[33] As Bauman's earlier had work suggested, sociology as a legislative vocation found its fullest expression in 'Durksonian' functionalism[34] – a hybrid incorporating the sociologies of Émile Durkheim and Talcott Parsons. For Bauman, the problem with Durkheimian sociology is that it understands society *sui generis*; that is it understands social behaviour as merely shaped by objective 'facts' external to individuals which need to be explained with recourse to other objective 'facts'. While the problem with Parsons is that although he attempted to provide for his own systems approach to sociology an action frame of reference – particularly in the book *The Structure of Social Action*[35] – in the event he still tended towards an ultimately deterministic approach to social action which he saw as being produced by the normative structure of the social system.

However, by now Bauman recognized that Marxism, too, by and large, not content with positing its own valuable contributions to sociology, tended to organize its ideas around grand, unified schemas, which tried to explain everything, contrary to the growing recognition that by the

1980s most people's faith in grand theory had collapsed and that there was no longer any room for big ideas.[36]

For all his criticisms of Marxism, Bauman would be the first to admit that its *doxa* (that is, the knowledge it thinks with, but not about) made perfectly good sense of the world under its own solidly modern, legislative terms of reference. However, with the transformation to liquid modernity, Marxism failed as a sociology because in common with other modern ideologies it attempted to impose on human experience monolithic hopes and dreams incompatible with its complexity and cultural variety.

Bauman's engagement with postmodernism was in full swing by the late 1980s and this had taught him to look at the already existing reality in a different way, to accept its ambivalence and contingencies as part of everyday life. He had not only become a rationalist who was not longer afraid to doubt reason but his work was now informed by a new kind of scepticism unknown to the certainty-seeking modern discourse of Marxism. As a result, Bauman recognized that it would no longer be ethical for him to be convinced by Marxism in the orthodox, legislating way. Yet this did not mean that he could not ponder about the world through a perspective he was no longer completely convinced by, but that he was now free to explore many other ways in which the 'story' of the world could be told, and in rejecting Marxism as a grand theory, he was now able to see both the past and the present of sociology through his own eyes.

Bauman was also no longer convinced by Marxism's goal of attaining equality of outcome. As Keith Tester's book *The Social Thought of Zygmunt Bauman* makes clear, the obvious link between the life and the work is in Bauman's sociology everywhere apparent and his own experiences of living with actually existing communism in Poland had taught him that Marxism did not really work in practice. Bauman also recognized in the lives of others less comfortable than his own some other legacies of actually existing communism which littered the path to freedom, such as the perpetuation of poverty. As Bauman was all too aware, the problem with actually existing Marxism was that it sought to achieve a society where doing and believing formed a solid unity in the form of communism, which came at much too high a cost because it was made at the expense of the freedom of the individual. And what was increasingly concerning him was his growing realization that if there are many beautiful ways of being human, how could the world ever be equal when it is full of such cultural variety?

What was increasingly dawning on Bauman was the recognition that equality might be a social good but it must always remain a slave to cultural difference. If cultural difference is the means and the mechanism by which humankind makes meaning and culture is everywhere and everything, it is also culture as praxis. In the event Bauman did not abandon his Marxist concern with inequality, but he was no longer convinced that the goal of equality should be a universal value. And the value that Bauman subsequently came to place above any other values in his sociology was the value of freedom[37] – the kind of freedom that allows human beings to achieve their individuality *de facto* rather than *de jure* and is, in the words of Isaiah Berlin,[38] *positive* rather than *negative*. In contemporary political speak, Bauman had become sceptical of third ways: it's either freedom or unfreedom. And for a person who had lived through unfreedom, he had learned from bitter experience that there is no third choice. In so doing, Bauman was not setting up a counter opposition between freedom and equality which was contrary to Marxism. On the contrary, he was simply suggesting that the former should wax towards the latter, and the latter should wane towards the former. In this sense, for Bauman Mark Two, the demise of academic Marxism simply evokes the cusp of society's metamorphosis from solid to liquid modernity.

Bauman and Marxism: a summary

In the end it would be best to describe Bauman's relationship with Marxism as ambivalent. For all the problems associated with Marxism's trademark brand of critical theory that, as we have seen, led him to the conclusion that it had got to the end of what it could do, we have also observed that his project was unwavering in its agreement with the Marxist project of human freedom and democracy – in spite of the fact that he could no longer reconcile this with accepting that every man and woman should be equal. We have also seen that Bauman Mark Two maintains a sociological approach that is socialist and therefore committed to praxis and to this extent, in common with Marxism, puts off 'until further notice' the completed Hegelian synthesis.[39] However, as we shall see in the next section, there is something more sinister about Marxism to which Bauman is antagonistic and which can be identified with its abiding characteristics as a perspective of what he would describe as the 'solid' modernist imagination: its appeal to Enlightenment standards of universal reason; its obsession with the social whole or the totality; its methodological reduction to science; its theoretical reduction to structural, economic and technological determinism; and its patrician disdain for alternatives.

UNDERSTANDING THE SOLID MODERNIST IMAGINATION: COMING TO TERMS WITH THE AMBIVALENCE OF MODERNITY

If much of Bauman's writing in the late 1980s had been spent coming to terms with the postmodern turn and the implications of this for developing an approach to sociology 'made to the measure' of liquid modernity, the beginning of the 1990s saw him mapping out a thoroughgoing critique of modernity. As I pointed out in Chapter One, sociologists only first began talking about the idea of modernity as a concept of significance with the emergence of theories of postmodernism and from this point modernity merged into a dialectic (modern versus postmodern) and the concept achieved a new independence. But what is meant by the concept of modernity?

It is not necessary here to provide a definitive discussion and anyway a detailed analysis is beyond the scope of this book. That said, the concept is pivotal to understanding Bauman's sociology, and before the discussion can begin some kind of answer must be given to this question. As Giddens has suggested, modernity 'refers to the modes of social life and organization which emerged in Europe from about the seventeenth century onwards and which subsequently became more or less worldwide in their influence'.[40] But if this definition tells us something about the timing of the historical emergence of modernity and its geographical location, it tells us little about its core institutional features and the *doxa* underpinning the modern way of understanding the world.

The idea of modernity, or I should say, modernization, refers to the emergence of a new faith in the processes of scientific knowledge and technological advance which marks the beginning of modernity's separation from traditional society. Giddens argues that, regardless of the initial force of circumstances that meant that it had to conspire with its progenitor, modernity contrives to destroy traditional society. For Giddens, tradition is a practice which is 'bound up with ... "collective memory"; involves ritual; is connected with ... a *formulaic notion of truth*; has "guardians"; and, unlike custom, has binding force which has a combined moral and emotional content'.[41] It is nigh on impossible to differentiate between real, invented and imagined traditions, but as Giddens shows, the formulaic *notion of the truth* of tradition is a manifestation of active 'collective memory'; and as such, is forever being recreated in the present. As Bauman suggests, traditional society was a relatively coherent society and constituted an organic totality of activities and knowledge which was fully integrated into everyday life.[42] Men and women did not merely populate their world in the modern sense; they were part of the world in which they lived and it was part of them.

Traditional society was lived in a ritualistic fashion and it constituted a communal way of life to the extent that it was thought of 'as *natural*, like other "facts of nature"; and it need not be laboriously constructed, maintained and serviced ... it is at its strongest and most secure when we believe just this: that we have not chosen it on purpose, have done nothing to make it exist and can do nothing to undo it'.[43]

In the modern sense, however, traditional life is *irrational*, without rules of reason: 'it is at once unchanging and arbitrary. Life must follow the ways of the past; and at the same time life cannot be planned ... patterns of life are fixed in ways that cannot, must not, be broken just because they are traditional; at the same time unpredictable, unreliable, miraculous'.[44] It is generally accepted that modernity, with the 'discovery' of some alternative 'universal laws' of nature and society, came into being with the Enlightenment and the shift from traditional society to modernity involved moving from a devotional religious world to a secular world of science.

Contrary to traditional society, with modernity, *rationality* becomes, in Giddens's sense, *embedded in* the knowledge process:

> intellectually calculable rules and procedures are increasingly substituted for sentiment, tradition and rule of thumb in all spheres of activity. Rationalisation leads to the displacement of religion by specialised science as the major source of intellectual authority; the substitution of the trained expert for the cultivated man of letters; the ousting of the skilled handworker by machine technology; the replacement of traditional judicial wisdom by abstract, systematic statutory codes. Rationalisation demystifies and instrumentalises life. It means that ... there are no mysterious, incalculable forces that come into play, but rather that one can, in principle, master all things by calculation.[45]

If traditional society was governed by predictability and certitude, modernity is inherently disorderly, experimental and go-getting. As Bauman puts it:

> *All* modernity means incessant, obsessive modernization (there is no state of modernity; only a process; modernity would cease being modernity the moment that process ground to a halt); and all modernization consists in 'disembedding', 'disencumbering', 'melting the solids', etc.; in other words, in dismantling the received structures or at least weakening their grip. From the start, modernity deprived the web of human relationships of its past holding force; 'disembedded' and set loose, humans were expected to seek new

beds and dig themselves in them using their own skills and resources, even if they chose to stay in the bed in which they germinated ('it is not enough to be a bourgeois', warned Jean-Paul Sartre; 'one needs to live one's life as a bourgeois').[46]

And with the coming of modernity it was expected – rather than merely hoped – that, with the accumulation of expert knowledge, rational science would supersede all irrational ways of understanding the world, and with the 'Death of God' modernity would now be able to resolve all the puzzles of the world. At long last, with a fulfilled Enlightenment, the masses would at last be freed from the shackles of the past.

The Enlightenment can be seen as an unprecedented political, social and cultural transformation, sustained by an unwavering and rationally charged intellectual energy which remade the world as modernity. This Enlightenment modernity was imbued with a progressivism which was concerned with unshackling the present and the future perfect from the problematic certainties of the past, in order to identify where change for the better was possible. The modern mindset was everything that the irrational predecessor was not, with its demand to classify things that hitherto had not been imagined as classifiable. And its central aim was to transmute the living reality into something that could be quantified. This led to the root-and-branch reform of all society's major institutions on the basis of taxonomy, or in other words, modules for classifying, recognizing and calculation. As Bauman points out, the modern taxonomy sensibility is that of the relentless tidier, for whom

nothing in the human condition is given once and for all and is imposed with no right of appeal or reform – that everything needs to be 'made' first and once made can be changed endlessly – accompanied the modern era from its beginning; indeed, obsessive and compulsive change (variously called 'modernizing', 'progress', 'improvement', 'development', 'updating') is the hard core of the modern mode of being.[47]

The shift to modernity must have felt like the greatest of all possible differences in the world. What was taking place in the emerging modernity was the experience of shift itself, the struggle of absolutists to put some definition, some finality, on what seemed to be an irrational world. In this sense, Bauman suggests that solid modernity was ambivalent from its inception because it involved a search for a new kind of permanence in a world that was destined to be the

age marked by constant change – but an age aware of being so marked; an age that views its own legal forms, its material and spiritual creations, its knowledge and convictions as temporary, to be held 'until further notice' and eventually disqualified and replaced by new and better ones. In other words, modernity is an era conscious of its own historicity. Human institutions are viewed as self-created and amenable to improvement; they can be retained only if they justify themselves in the face of stringent demands of reason – and if they fail the test, they are bound to be scrapped. The substitution of new designs for old will be a progressive move, a new step up the ascending line of human development.[48]

What was also apparent with modernity was that from its inception it sparked other kinds of reactions, such as nostalgia for the idea of traditional community, which could be understood as an accurate if not a paradigmatic measure of the disdain for modernity found in some intellectual movements. As the community studies literature shows, from the publication of Tönnies classic book *Gemeinschaft und Gesellschaft* (*Community and Society*)[49] at least, this resistance to modernity was also steadfastly located in the quotidian lives of ordinary individuals through the re-emergence of modern community groupings and latter-day involvement in social movements.

The solid modernist imagination

As one commentator has put it, during the early onset of modernity the Enlightenment lost some of its impetus but it was to make 'a spectacular comeback by transforming itself into an all conquering Modernity and expanding to colonize the globe'.[50] Agnes Heller[51] suggests that from the middle of the 19th century onwards there had been established in Europe and thereafter the New World what could be described as a high modernist version of modernity or what Bauman in his work after *Liquid Modernity* would refer to as the solid modernist imagination. What was distinctive about the emergence of this solid modern imagination was its curiosity about the individual, and the future perfect of the world outside individuals, which came to be valued more than any renewed conversation with the past. The onset of modernity was perceived not only as the cusp of change, but the moment when history had at last begun and its protagonists had their eyes firmly planted on the future in 'the search for the state of perfection, a state that puts paid to all further change, having first made change uncalled-for and undesirable. All further change would be for the worse.'[52]

The solid modern imagination also looked for a reason for everything and it was this dynamic that was the impetus behind the emergence of science as the dominant discourse of modernity. Accordingly, solid modernity was characterized by scientific 'projects' which were to be fulfilled in the future. The discourse underpinning such projects was itself characterized by a calculative drive which drew on different forms of classification in order to give the world a structure. Drawing on the work of Cornelius Castoriadis, Bauman suggests that every society conjures up its own imaginary through which it legitimizes its activities and institutions, that when established follows a unifying logic[53] through which the society in question – in Foucault's terminology – effectively discursively constitutes itself; that is establishes its *autonomy* through a pattern of intuitional frameworks across a number of sites. As a number of scholars have suggested, the foremost sites through which 19th-century modern societies established their autonomy were industrialism, capitalism and the nation-state. What is of substantive concern to Bauman in this regard, and something he shares with a number of thinkers from Weber to Foucault, is their preoccupation with the way in which the institution of the autonomous realm of solid modernity saw it hastily turning its impetus away from Enlightenment liberation to new and more efficient means of social control.

Modernity and social control

As Bauman makes clear, the solid modernist imaginary was that of unabashed system building, a world view after establishing first principles and foundations, and its central organizing theme was social engineering.[54] First, it assumed that the direction that the modern world would develop would be motivated by human hands rather than natural processes and that this direction would to a large extent be guided towards a society in which work would be subject to ever-growing efficiency and would be based on a detailed division of labour and increasing expertise. Second, and related to these processes, there would be a growing harmonization of needs which would arise from the 'efficient management of society as a whole and the springs of individual action'. Consequently, with this progress to more rationality, people would opt for efficient and effective action over inadequate knowledge or misinformation. Thirdly, and related to the above, there would develop a correspondence between the representations of what constitutes social reality with science. In a nutshell, science would eventually not only help society to better manage its social affairs, but it would also leave it better equipped to uncover and demystify the truths about social reality.

As I have suggested already, classification was a modern outlook which appealed to Enlightenment standards of universal reason. And with its passion for taxonomy, modernity was typically corrective and exacting, revising and adjusting particular phenomena to its relentless normalizing discourse. As Bauman argues, once forged, modernity's coin quickly became the common currency and all aspects of life had to get their required doses of its classifying zeal in order to guarantee their legitimacy. In the event, public life and private life came to be understood as distinct spheres of social life and the knowledge process was likewise separated into specialized realms.

As Bauman's theory of solid modernity implies, there was no necessary reason why modernity should have taken the normalizing course that it did, because although Enlightenment thinking appealed to standards of universal reason it also signified a resistance to absolutism. But as he suggests, the solid modernist version of modernity as it was discursively constituted in actually existing nation-states tended to be underpinned by a system of social control that not only classified but also understood any form of deviation from its norms of classification as a thorn in its flesh. As Bauman points out:

> Modern society differs from its predecessors by its gardener-like, rather than gamekeeper-like, attitude to itself. It views the maintenance of social order (i.e. the containment of human conduct within certain parameters, and the predictability of human behaviour within these parameters) as an 'issue': something to be kept on the agenda, considered, discussed, taken care of, dealt with, resolved.[55]

In the event, modern societies found that an effective way of maintaining social order was to compare human conduct with certain regularities from the past, which allowed them to establish systems of social control whereby they could identify different behaviours from a particular point of view in order to predict the future. In this way the modern outlook on the one hand implied 'historical awareness, a consciousness of historical continuity and the ways the past continues to live in the present'.[56] (As Agnes Heller points out, modern people are the first people to understand what history is really about, because it is science which enables them to understand the puzzles of the past.) On the other hand, it was science which also enabled them to predict the future, as Bauman suggests, to predict human behaviour within 'certain parameters'.

It was imagined that the power of this kind of reasoning that allowed modern 'man' to 'make a world of his own design and liking', would be assuaged by the disciplinary rules of empirical experience which would provide the separation between the 'form' and the 'content' of knowledge. Science, whose central appeal and strength was based on the positivistic observation of the 'world out there', was seen as ideal for making this linkage. However, if this meant that the rules of perfect reason would be tempered by the rules of empirical experience developed through scientific experimentation, it did not stop the attitude to certainty associated with the old way of life being made compatible with the new one.

Freud suggested as much in the first section of his famous essay *Civilisation and Its Discontents*, when he took Rome to be a useful metaphor for the processes of modern civilization. Like Rome, Freud suggested, modernity might be evolving towards a newer and better society but it could not entirely shake off its past. Modernity carries with it, beneath its modern foundations, the ambivalence of its own historicity. As Freud put it, 'nothing which has once been formed can perish – that everything is somehow preserved and that in suitable circumstances (when, for instance, regression goes back far enough) it can once more be brought to light'.[57] What Freud's analysis suggests is that at one level there was with solid modernity the *progressive* affirmation of beauty, cleanliness and order; but at another it had 'buried in the soil of its city or beneath its modern buildings'[58] the *regressive* means of power and social control for their implementation.

Modernity and the Holocaust: the solid modern way of dealing with contingency and ambivalence

In *Modernity and the Holocaust*, Bauman demonstrates that this tyranny associated with this 'dark' side of modern culture was inextricably linked to the modern obsession with cleanliness and order, particularly when cultural ambivalence became a problem and its elimination turned into a mission.[59] As Bauman suggests in *Postmodern Ethics*, making sure there is a 'distance rather than *proximity* ... between the perpetrator of an action and those who suffer its consequences'[60] is of utmost importance here since it allows the perpetrator to construct the sufferers as 'the objective of aesthetic, not moral evaluation; as a matter of taste, not responsibility';[61] and their exemption 'from the class of individuals worthy of moral respect; [while] "dissembling" ... human beings [in this case the Jews] into functionally specific traits, each of which has a discreet technical utility that precludes any moral response to the individual as an expressive and vulnerable alterity'.[62]

As Bauman shows in *Modernity and the Holocaust*, this denial of proximity was most acutely represented in the Holocaust. Contrary to many other critics, Bauman understands the Holocaust as a 'solidly' modern 'project', essentially a Fordist[63] mass-production genocide which was the *fait accompli* of the solid modern imagination, the style and the substance of which could only have been realized in modernity. If its style of execution was technological, the substance of the 'final solution' was to once and for all rid the world of those 'aliens' distorting its reality in order to uncover the 'true' nature of humankind. As Bauman points out, 'the state of affairs the Nazis wished to create was one of total *Entfernung* – an effective removal of the Jews from the life-world of the German race'.[64] Be that as it may, as David Macey has suggested, Bauman insists that the Holocaust was

> neither a 'Jewish problem' nor a 'German' problem', nor, *contra* Adorno, the expression of an authoritarian personality … [but] it was a project born of and implemented in a modern rational society. Modern civilization was not the Holocaust's sufficient cause, but it was one of its necessary causes. Rational bureaucracy, scientific planning and scientific rationality in the service of absolute modern power created it.[65]

As the same author goes on to point out, 'understanding the Holocaust is an essential task of any theory of modernity' and what Bauman does in *Modernity and the Holocaust* is demonstrate at both a theoretical and empirical level George Santayana's memorable point that there is tragedy in all attempts to find perfection, because the world in which perfection arises is itself imperfect. In other words, the real world unlike the imaginary world will always be imperfect because it is guided by the contingency events which always involve human choices. To put it another way, ambivalence – and this is Bauman's brilliant point – is the creature of modernity. But the problem with the solid modern imagination was that it stumbled on contingency and narrated it as a will to order rather than accepting its ambivalence. In terms of the Holocaust, Nazi Germany chose to understand the wonderful quality of human 'untidiness' as something it needed to cure the world of and the appeal of the Holocaust was that it was perceived that it would allow its perpetrators to expunge the ambivalence of the Jewish race from the imaginative space of the future perfect of modern German humanity.

EXCURSUS – DECONSTRUCTING THE SOLID MODERN IMAGINATION: THE METAPHOR OF THE RAILWAY STATION[66]

In the solid modernist imagination, the present of the already existing reality – the life-world of the here and now – is like a railway station where modern people go to catch their trains to the future. As I have suggested above, the onset of solid modernity was perceived not only as the cusp of change, but also as the moment when history had at last begun and its protagonists had their eyes firmly planted on the future. From the outlook of the solid modernist imagination, the world of the present is understood as merely a temporary stopping-off point. It is seen as temporary because the solid modernist imagination imagines that stopping off in any one place for too long is a pointless business – the place to be is in the future. This is because for the solid modernist imagination the future is understood as that inestimable place that is the province of freedom: the future perfect.

Bauman swerves from the invitation of looking at the future. He accepts life on the railway station. He is content to let life be lived in the here and now; he has no expectations of the future perfect. From Bauman's outlook, all dreams of the future perfect are ambivalent in their consequences and his life experiences have taught him as much. The two solid modernist dreams of the future perfect most close to his identity are the Holocaust and the experience of living in actually existing communism in Poland. The former taught him that technological progress might have created security and prosperity for some groups of people, but it brought insecurity and human destruction for others, while the 'success' of the latter was realized through the imposition of bureaucracy and the expulsion of those opposed to its absolutist objectives. Indeed, the names of the terminal railway stations to which these two examples of the solid modernist imagination headed were not 'freedom' and 'emancipation', but 'Auschwitz' and the 'Gulag' – two railway stations of extermination. To reiterate, Bauman's point is that through its own self-deception the solid modernist imagination stumbled on contingency and chose not to take into consideration the consciousness of its ambivalence – it chose instead to narrate it as order.

Consequently, in his sociology Bauman implores us to dig into all dreams of the future perfect and ask what they mean, and he suggests that without exception holes will begin to appear; all models of the future perfect are bound to be suspect. All stories of finality should be distrusted, because like all other stories they cannot help but be shot through with ambivalence. Bauman asks us to claim ignorance in matters of final destination and to accept the here and now for what it is. Bauman himself accepts the contingency of the present; he accepts the 'untidy' ambivalence of humanity. As a result, Bauman is not going to portray for us solid figures with vices and virtues painted upon them in his sociology. He is going to chart for us the trajectories of lives made real by the contingency and ambivalence of events. This is why Bauman prompts us to recognize that love and hate, good and evil can exist anywhere. As Peter Beilharz has put it, he knows that 'human actors are capable of this, and the other'.[67]

This does not mean that for Bauman anything goes. On the contrary, it means that living on the railway station of the present presents him with the opportunity to make a choice between responsibility and taking shelter from responsibility. Bauman suggests that the challenge facing all men and women today is not finding the next cure for ambivalence but about taking responsibility for the consciousness of contingency. Bauman's message to his readers is this: only by living in the present moment – rather than the future – will they be able to escape from it; by accepting contingency, find constancy; by letting themselves go, pull themselves together.

To this end Bauman is concerned with the opposition between *responsibility* and *bystanding* in his sociology. In other words, accepting that one lives on the railway station of the present is a matter of choice between taking individual responsibility for one's actions or *bystanding* and 'taking shelter where responsibility for one's action need not be taken by the actors'.[68] So instead of offering any ready-made guidelines for living, Bauman merely offers us in his work an orientation, with strong moral and political undercurrents, which, if it cannot base its truths on foundational criteria, can resolve itself to try to be always *responsible*. In this sense, what Bauman is offering us is the basis of a life-strategy which is an indictment of those *bystanders* whose actions and complicity perpetuate oppression and exploitation in order to limit human freedom.

FROM SOLID MODERNITY TO LIQUID MODERNITY

For Bauman, the waning of the solid modern imagination began once it dawned on modern men and women that the 'grand experiment of modernity'[69] had not lived up to the expectations of those who promulgated the triumph of rational Enlightenment over tradition. And as far as Bauman is concerned the evidence of this can be found everywhere in our everyday lives, not only at the terminal railway stations marked 'Auschwitz' and 'Gulag'. The idea of liquid modernity emerges from the point where solid modernity begins to contemplate itself. According to Bauman, liquid modernity is solid modernity 'coming to terms with its own impossibility; a self-monitoring modernity, one that consciously discards what it was once unconsciously doing'.[70] Following in the footsteps of Weber's classic analysis[71] of the emergence of industrial capitalism from traditional society, Bauman also presumes that liquid modernity and solid modernity form an interlacing contrast, and that neither can be discussed in isolation.

It is in the book *Memories of Class* that Bauman first begins to differentiate between solid modernity and liquid modernity – figuratively if not literally – when, as I have suggested already, he argues that consumption and consumer culture were taking on the central role in the economy that had once been the privilege of production and work. However, at this point in his writing Bauman was still struggling to find the most adequate way of articulating what is perhaps the most difficult problem facing the sociologist who has in his work, consciously or not, set about dismantling the hierarchical binary opposites that continue to nag orthodox sociology: how to set up a useful and meaningful comparison without falling into the trap of devaluing one in favour of the other. The other problem facing him was his knowledge of what Alexis de Tocqueville also understood perfectly well: that 'without comparisons to make, the mind does not know how to proceed'.[72]

In the event Bauman took a leaf out of the book of another great sociologist, Max Weber, who had also been preoccupied with 'the difficulties involved in constructing an explanation of a unique historical phenomenon that would be adequate on the levels both of 'meaning' and of empirical verification'.[73] Especially from *Legislators and Interpreters* onward he began to adopt an 'ideal-typical' kind of analysis which also had affinities with the *Annales School* in its recognition of the different durations of historical time: the *longue durée* of modernity itself, but more particularly the intermediate rate of change associated with *conjoncture* time, which he was now using when he distinguished between modernity and postmodernity and thereafter solid modernity and liquid modernity.

In his use of ideal-types Bauman also recognized Weber's argument that they are merely abstract idealizations constructed from a *particular point of view*.[74] However, of the range of means Bauman now had for giving himself something to say, his use of ideal-typical analysis proved to be one of the most effective, because it enabled him to hold the 'solid' dimension of the problem of modernity constant, so that he could establish the differences along the 'liquid' modern other. In developing such an approach to sociology, Bauman was not oblivious to the same problem that Max Weber had to grapple with in his work: in the final analysis ideal-types probably 'tell us less about social reality than about the inbuilt preconceptions of the investigator'.[75] However, unlike Weber, Bauman recognized that sociology can never be 'value-free' activity and that the biography of the sociologist is inexorably bound up with the social reality he makes in his analyses. Bauman's work is an indictment of the kind of sociology that avoids emotional conviction and an examination of his biography confirms this standpoint.

As Bauman has said, we must recognize that in reality we do not live in either solid modernity or liquid modernity. Both of these 'worlds' are 'but abstract idealizations of mutually incoherent aspects of the single life-process which we all try our best to make as coherent as we can manage. Idealizations are no more (but no less either) than sediments, and also indispensable tools, of those efforts'.[76] This is reflected in Bauman's recognition that the illustrative force of these concepts is far from complete (after all, who are we to talk of the certainty and relative stability of times in which we did not live?), and in his confidence that we must recognize not only contrasts but also a degree of overlap between the two, a seeping of the 'solid' into the 'liquid' other. Yet Bauman's picture of this juxtaposition is also a critical reminder of a 'solid' modern world that was, but is no longer, ours.

Bauman suggests that, over the last 100 years, solid modernity, the *conjoncture* stage of order-seeking in the face of increasing disorder, has gradually been transformed into a liquid modernity which entails living 'without an ultimate, perfect model of society, [where] individual life reflects the experience of being in an increasingly "deregulated", or – as the politicians' beloved cliché has it – *flexible* world: a world full of uncoordinated, often contradictory chances and voices, but devoid of clear-cut standards by which the superiority of any of them can he measured'.[77] Bauman argues that liquid modernity means living in a world where social relationships are continually up for grabs because they are constantly being made, undone and remade. For Bauman, as for Agnes Heller, liquid modern men and women 'think and act as if everything … were entirely contingent in the strongest sense of the word (without plan, necessity, tendency, and so on), but do not speak of contingency … A contingent person simply acts and lives with the consciousness of con-tingency'.[78] Drawing on Anthony Giddens's idea that social relationships are 'disembedded' or 'lifted out' of local contexts and remade across time and space,[79] Bauman argues that liquid modernity is best understood as 'the continuation of disembedding coupled with dis-continuation of re-embedding. The latter, once the prime goal of [the solid] modernising bustle, is these days no more on offer, and shunned'.[80]

The transition from solid modernity to liquid modernity is, however, perhaps best summed up in his reversal of Freud's idea that solid modernity was only able to maintain its *status quo* as long as people by and large accepted the normalizing constraints of the 'reality principle'. Writing over 70 years ago, Freud[81] argued that in solid modernity the majority of people lived their lives largely content that their desires to transgress the dominant moral order should remain at the level of fantasy, mainly because they were prepared to surrender their individual freedoms for the sake of more *Sicherheit*, a composite German expression which

Bauman uses to capture the collective self-assurance that people have when they experience their lives as certain, secure and safe.

According to Bauman, however, in liquid modernity 'the balance has shifted away from Freud's "too little freedom in exchange for more security"'[82] and today individuals set out to live their lives not so much as *desires* built on the premise that the unlived life is the only life worth living,[83] so much as a lived life where they make their *wishes* come true, but in the process surrender 'a lot of *Sicherheit* in exchange for fewer constraints on freedom of choice and self-expression'.[84] Bauman's sociology recognizes that we have shifted from a more structured society in which identity was largely ascribed by social class (and gender and ethnicity) to a sociality in which individuality dominates more than anything else, and where identity always remains a work in progress and is largely achieved through consumption – a sociality in which life is lived *noch nicht* surrounded by possibilities that have not yet been realized. In such a sociality self-transformation is not just a possibility – it is a duty.

But as Bauman goes on to point out, we should not understand liquid modernity as a world lacking in purpose or values. On the contrary, he argues that living in liquid modernity 'is an experience of a world overflowing with a multitude of tempting and seductive possibilities and haunted by the excess of values worth pursing. Such an experience is both stimulating and unnerving – it may stir into action as well as paralyse, exhilarate or cause despair'.[85] With regard to the values that liquid moderns live their lives by, Bauman argues that whereas solid modernity tended to be close-minded when it sought to promote its moral codes as universally valid, liquid modernity provides an opportunity for moral responsibility proper, which 'is the most personal and inalienable of human possessions, and the most precious of human rights'.[86]

CONCLUSIONS

What I have demonstrated in this chapter is that in the sociology he was developing from the late 1980s onwards, Bauman, in the spirit of his literary hero, Jorge Luis Borges, was not so much rejecting Marxism as challenging its contingencies and tacit assumptions in order to imagine it again. Just as the project of Borges's protagonist Pierre Menard is to create his own *Don Quixote*[87] without the legislating truth claims of Cervantes, so Bauman's major publications in the 1980s and 1990s set out to prove that as a sociologist he could develop his own interpretive theory of modernity without necessarily being Karl Marx. In this regard, his main idea was to show that as the world moves on, sociologists read it in different ways and that these readings provide valuable new insights and interpretations that critical theorists such as Marx, writing in the context of 19th-century modernity, could not have anticipated. In effect he recast Marx's solid and absolute tale in an elastic and fragmenting liquid modern deconstruction.

In the process of developing his own alternative position, Bauman recognized too that his own story of modernity – the story of a mere sociologist who was trying to anticipate what Marx could not have anticipated – would have to take its place amongst countless other stories about modernity. This does not mean that Bauman was suggesting that after Marx anything can pass as a great story, just that in the light of what he had learned from deconstructing both Marxism and the idea of modernity he came to recognize, like Borges, that even if we cannot guarantee in advance which stories will work and which will not, there will only be a few that will be really forceful, only a few that will be really convincing.

However, Bauman also recognized that he would not be able to justify his alternative story of modernity in the rationalist, legislative way of Marxism, by spelling out beforehand the criteria by which his work should be assessed. He recognized that his story of modernity, like Pierre Menard's *Don Quixote*, would have to succeed on the basis of its own merits; it would have to have relevance for its readers. Bauman recognized too that he would not be able to claim that he was following the 'correct' methodological procedures, but he knew he would still be able to claim quality and rigour for his work if he could show that his theory of modernity worked better than Marx's.

We can therefore conclude that Bauman has learned from his own personal voyage of discovery that after Marx the challenge for the sociologist is to tell stories about modernity that work, but without claiming for them absolute truth or closure in the ways and means of the solid modernist imagination. We can also conclude that Bauman's own sociological project is unavoidably ambivalent. On the face of it, it seems as if its author has conjured up for us his own story of modernity which to all intents and purposes resembles what Lyotard calls a grand narrative.[88] But to see Bauman's sociology as a grand narrative would be inaccurate. This is because its author remains true to his scepticism of absolutes and composes for us a stunning sonata instead of a last symphony. Bauman's is a project which is conceived by someone who apparently wants to paint for us a total picture of a broken totality, or more accurately, a fragmented world. But this picture can't be a grand narrative because the artist in question knows from personal experience the dangerous ground where totalizing brushstrokes take you.

As a sociology of liquid modernity, Bauman's project can never be a totalizing system because it recognizes that just as the world is contingent, ambivalent and infinitely various, so is sociology. In this sense, Bauman is neither a naïve essentialist nor a relativist and he understands that sociologists – like the liquid modern men and women whose lives they attempt to understand – can no longer hope to put together any decisive truth about the world 'out there' in the legislative meaning. Bauman knows that it is wrong to have an ideal view of the world and in his sociology he is not making universal truths claims, but instead merely asking his readers to join him and take his word in assuming certain things are 'true' and if he and his readers can inspire some critical dialogue, they will also have accomplished something along the way. Just as importantly, however, he understands that the one thing that all men and women living today hold in common is their shared sense of this fragmented world, and it is his ability to grasp this penetrating insight that makes his sociology 'made to the measure' of liquid modern times. It is with men and women's life strategies for coping with this fragmented world that Chapter Four is devoted, but before that we must consider the ways and means of Bauman's sociology.

3

The Ways and Means of the Dragoman

> With his self-confidence Bauman is not bothered too much by the boundaries between politics, social science and cultural history; social-psychological analysis and existential reflections inter-mingle; he switches back and forth between literary and logical expositions; he changes the lenses from hermeneutical to systematical, analytical and back: finally his moral philosophy searches for indeterminacy beyond all definitions. All these combinations match his conception of sociology.
>
> Peter Nijhoff[1]

In the light of what has been discussed in the previous chapter and as the above quotation suggests, the reader will be beginning to grasp that the phenomenon that is Zygmunt Bauman does not fit into the carefully organized classificatory academic divisions that are the mainstay of the modern university system. It is perhaps odd then that he may go down in history as the last great sociologist, when as Nijhoff suggests, the ways and means of his sociology hardly ever adhere to orthodox sociological conventions, to the extent that his position as a sociologist becomes over time ever more difficult to sustain. But if Bauman's sociological approach is rather different to what sociology might expect of one of its major protagonists, it is still true to the idea of sociology as praxis. Indeed, as stressed at the beginning of this book, Bauman follows Marx's dictum that it is not enough for the sociologist to study society; he also needs to change it.

It is because of his commitment to sociology as praxis that Bauman jabs with the speed of a prize fighter in developing his critical analyses which seldom – if ever – miss their targets and like all great pugilists he works his craft like poetry in motion. The sociology can be described as such precisely because of its author's use of imaginative word play, his use of startling metaphors and juxtapositions, and not least because of its overall poetic effects. As the reader will see, Bauman's is a way of doing sociology that is characterized more by passion than exactitude, by imagination rather than by order, and by literature rather than social science. What Alan Malachowski has said of Richard Rorty's philosophy is true of Bauman's sociology: he wants it to live side by side in a fruitful interaction with art.[2] In this chapter, I argue that significantly Bauman promotes sociology as an art of hermeneutic relevance, requiring of its pretenders not only the inspired *and* practical exercise of the sociological imagination but a way of social theorizing that is morally responsible.

Despite the paradigmatic significance of Bauman's special way of practising sociology, students will find nothing written about its ways and means in the pages of the introductory textbooks. One reason for this is that Bauman himself has had very little to say about issues of methodology. And if you were to ask him about the place of methodology in his sociology he would not be interested. Instead he would probably reply that his job simply involves getting on with the task of interpreting and providing an appropriate critique of what he calls the 'mechanism and momentum' of the contemporary world. This is not unsurprising because it is what he is good at and what really interests him. However, that Bauman is not interested in issues of methodology is hardly a convincing explanation for the lack of attention given to how he does sociology.

What I want to argue in this chapter is that the textbooks continue to remain silent on the kind of sociology Bauman practises because it does not offer a methodology as such but an *orientation* to inquiry with strong moral and political undercurrents. The problem with this kind of inquiry for sociology is that it is unable to contemplate the radical significance of what it might actually entail for sociology itself. As Bauman himself has suggested, sociology has long had a problem of confronting head-on the question of its own value. Writing in response to Anthony Giddens's[3] attempt to incorporate into sociology some *New Rules of Sociological*

Method, Bauman suggested that the problem with these 'new rules' is that they remained part of the crisis sociology was attempting to break away from. In Bauman's words

> rules of method are an internal affair of sociology, part of its power rhetoric and of a pep talk turned upon itself; [and they] … tell us little about the subject-matter of sociology; moreover, in no way do they contain a guarantee that sociology would have something valid and relevant to say on this subject.[4]

In concluding his critique of Giddens's prognosis, Bauman suggested that what is most wrong with sociology today is that it continues to try to make sense of 'society' with the concepts that have been around since the inception of orthodox sociology without recognizing that the trouble with these concepts is that most of them do not work as well as they once did.

Bauman is most certainly a sociologist of suspicion, but he is not a 'gravedigger of the present', to use an aphorism from Nietzsche. He may think that there are many problems with sociology but he remains its biggest fan and sees its future as guaranteed, precisely because of its ability to tell our truths much better than any other academic discipline. And as he clearly recognizes, if it has had some difficulties in finding a part and a purpose for some new concepts in its lexicon, sociology has been more successful in developing its theoretical orientations because of its plural nature and its ability to soak up ideas from a range of complementary and alternative disciplines. This means that sociology is always on the look out for new and innovative ways of understanding the world and it, according to Bauman, is better placed than any other discipline to understand the social world as a felt reality. As he puts it:

> Whatever the spokesmen for sociology may say about the nature of their work, sociology is an ongoing dialogue with human experience, and that experience, unlike the university buildings is not divided into departments, let alone tightly sealed departments. Academics may refuse or neglect to read their next floor or neigh-bours' work and so carry unscathed conviction of their own separate identity, but this cannot be said of human experience, in which the sociological, political, the economic, the philosophical, the psychological, the historical, the poetic and what not are blended to the extent that no single ingredient can salvage its substance or identity in case of separation. I would go as far as to say that however hard it may try, sociology would never win the 'war of independ-ence'. More to the point, it would never survive a victorious

outcome of such a war, were it at all conceivable. The discursive formation bearing the name of sociology is porous on all sides and is a notorious, enormous, insatiable, absorptive power. Personally, I believe that this is sociology's strength not weakness. I believe that the future of sociology is assured precisely because it comes nearer than any other academic discipline to embracing human experience in its entirety.[5]

It will become apparent in the following pages that it is Bauman himself who is the custodian of this plural view of sociology, the major representative of a multi-faceted faith which any one particular viewpoint could only impoverish. As for sociology itself, I want to argue that, although it has experienced nothing less than a theoretical revolution – particularly over the last twenty years or so – to the extent that it has witnessed the emergence of a number of divergent trends in its ranks, it is largely the case that their combined input has not been used to confront the putative assumptions that underpin the orthodox sociological way of understanding the world. I also want to argue that this carries some precarious consequences for social theorizing today, which can be understood in terms of the constraints that sociology continues to place on the alternative ways of seeing the world that it incorporates into the discursive formation of sociology itself, and the significance of this tendency for the problems deriving from that place. The argument I develop in this chapter is that it is the mark of an ever-changing discursive formation of sociology that it paradoxically continues to develop a way of thinking that insists on the ability of sociological analysis to correspond with the already existing reality, which ironically is merely a reiteration of what it seems to have been doing since its inception as an academic discipline.

THE AMBIVALENCE OF SOCIOLOGY

In Bauman's sense, it can be argued that if the sociological landscape is destined to undergo incessant change, at the current time sociology confronts this state of affairs in a way that is ambivalent through and through; amid the massive profusion of theoretical influences that sociology has readily soaked up, and continues to soak up at an exponential rate – from cultural studies, poststructuralism, postmodernism, queer theory, to name but a few – it has been reluctant to offer or acknowledge any radically alternative ways of *practising* sociology. Although the ideas of postmodernism and poststructuralism and particularly the work of thinkers such as Foucault and Derrida, for example, have had a profound *theoretical* influence on sociology, they have not impacted in any decisive ways on the cognitive frames through which most sociologists *think* about the social world and how they *go about* the task of researching that world. If most people in sociology today are not naive enough to make the assumption that the meticulous and gradual observation of social phenomena provides a grounding for theory *vis-à-vis* Glaser and Strauss,[6] they do nonetheless make the grave error of presuming that theory and empirical evidence provide a continuum without which sociology cannot persist. I want to suggest that what we have with this trend is a kind of positivism in sociology that is so relentless in its pursuit of empirical truths that it renders other alternatives as extraneous. And this is the major reason why the ways and means of Bauman's sociology are never contemplated in the sociology textbooks.

Those who wish to observe this dialectic in action need look no further than in the pages of the sociology journals and the PowerPoint slides at the sociology conferences. It cannot be denied that sociology has some inventive and talented theorists, but their writing is in the main still rooted in a 'data-discourse', the coercive rhetoric of the scientific orthodoxy that remains the prevailing paradigm for sociology-speak. The same can be said about the ways in which sociology tends to incorporate alternative ways of understanding the actually existing reality. Time and again sociologists apply the ideas of Foucault *et al.* to empirical research projects which use ethnography, interviews, and sometimes even surveys and questionnaires, without recognizing that if poststructuralism comes in a range of varieties, each rejects the cosy, humanized 'commonsense' notions of what sociology takes for granted about the relationship between the research process and understanding the actually existing reality. That poststructuralist thinking is anti-humanist, anti-realist and anti-foundationalist in orientation, dealing with anti-social signs, language, writing and deconstruction (Derrida), and archaeology and genealogy (Foucault) is simply lost on many sociologists.[7]

What is the reason for this ambivalent state of affairs? Following Richard Rorty,[8] I want to argue that once sociology recognized Bauman's point that it was no longer – if it ever was – a solitary discipline of its own kind, it was also confronted with the issue of addressing the distinction between necessary and contingent truths. What I mean by this is the idea that although the discursive formation known as sociology was now happy to soak up seemingly endless different ways of interpreting the world suggested by theories such as poststructuralism and post-modernism, it could not, and still cannot, imagine any cognitive frames and, by implication, methodological frameworks, other than those informed by orthodox sociological ways of thinking, because these might render many, if not all, of its own prevailing beliefs about the world as falsely drawn.

Consequently, there is a sentence from Nietzsche which hangs over sociology today: 'I fear we are not getting rid of God because we still believe in grammar'. What I mean by belief in grammar is the widespread conviction in sociology that its tried and tested theories and methods somehow presuppose an order of things, which mirrors its conviction that it has a ready-made way of conceptualizing the already existing reality which is more adequate than any other. I want to suggest that when confronted with what Rorty calls 'foreigners'' alternative cognitive frames, rather than changing its grammar, sociology merely *translates* their contents into its own language rather than trying to imagine what those cognitive frames might mean for sociology if they remained as *untranslatable* languages.

The truth of the matter is that complacency is spread like treacle on the epistemological outlook of sociology to the extent that what it finds difficult is not only separating what it *now* knows from what it *used* to know, but also admitting to itself that what it *now* knows can tell it a great deal about how sociologists themselves should go about understanding a world that has changed in profound ways. In a nutshell, the ways and means of understanding the actually existing reality that sociology continues to opt for, go against the grain of many of the new theoretical insights that it is working with. And rather than incorporate changes in its *doxa* it seems as if sociology is destined to spend its foreseeable future merely repainting the world in the black and white of its own worn-out terms of reference.

As that most acerbic of cultural commentators, Roland Barthes, might have put it: because sociology fails to reread its own tacit terms of reference it is obliged to read the same story everywhere. Following Bauman,[9] my point is that if sociology's *doxa* was founded in its formative years, this endowment still maintains a kind of constitutional status, despite infusions of theoretical insights from a wide range of perspectives. And the upshot is that sociology still expects the already existing reality to reflect itself in its own model of 'society', a kind of metaphysics – in Nietzsche's meaning, a logically consistent view of the world with its own God as part of that view. Consequently, as Bauman might say, it has a tendency to 're-paint the world's portrait' in its own mind's eye. This is the irony of sociology today, that while its ability to absorb myriad theories and concepts from a diversity of other disciplines signifies that it is in one sense a healthy discipline – not least because it is marked by a resistance to absolutism – its methodological imagination is characteristically conservative and corrective, reworking and fine-tuning what it soaks up to fit its own narrow epistemological outlook. In other words, what I am suggesting is that, in Bauman's terms, sociology's self-consciousness about its own modernity is not palpable; and by refusing to ask the impossible question about its own value, sociology puts into doubt its continuing relevance to those whom it claims to speak.

And it is sociology's inability to address the ambivalence of its own relevance which renders the textbooks unable to provide students with some ready-made guidelines for understanding the ways and means of Bauman's sociology. Following Rorty, Bauman realizes that the point of sociology is not to bring discourse to a close, but to perpetuate it in ever-more interesting ways – unfortunately sociology does not. To paraphrase that most insightful of historiographers, Hayden White, in my view, sociology is in a bad shape today, because it has lost sight of its affiliations in the literary imagination. In the interests of *appearing* scientific and objective, it represses and denies to itself its own greatest source of strength and renewal. By drawing sociology to a more intimate connection with its literary basis, we should not only be putting ourselves on guard against *merely* ideological distortions; we should also be by the way of arriving at that 'theory' of sociology without which it cannot pass for a 'discipline' at all.[10]

As Bauman might say, sociology can only be transformed once it begins to contemplate itself; when it comes to terms with its own impossibility and consciously discards what it is unconsciously doing.[11] What I demonstrate in the rest of this discussion is that buried amongst the pages of Bauman's stupendous output is not merely a revealing critique of sociology, but also – and most importantly for the purposes of this chapter – some lesson plans for going about the task of learning foreign languages, so that sociology can 'repaint the world's portrait' in colour rather than being prepared to accept it in monochrome. As Goethe once observed, 'when one learns a foreign language, one acquires a new country'. As the reader will have already begun to grasp, in his sophisticated scholarship Bauman has made a lot of countries his own and as I show in this chapter his sociology is an ongoing commentary on how to absorb foreign languages and draw new strength from their energy and enterprise.

As Angus Bancroft[12] has said, Bauman 'points to a path for a sociology that has lost its way', which in Richard Rorty's terms can be understood as the task of 'redescribing' sociology. If Bauman's critique of sociology is not as scathing as my own, he does recognize that it is, to paraphrase Rorty, caught in a contest between an entrenched vocabulary which has become a nuisance and a half-formed vocabulary which vaguely promises great things.[13] He recognizes, too, that if we want to argue convincingly for a new way of understanding the world, but we recognize that we cannot resort to any foundational criteria for justifying that our version of the world is better than anybody else's, we must set about convincing people to suspend their own favoured positions and take our word in assuming certain things are 'true'; and then we can succeed in getting some good sociological work done.

As I demonstrate in the following pages, by redescribing sociology through the literary imagination, Bauman is not only able to jettison much of the positivistic intellectual baggage that continues to undermine the potential of sociology, but in the process he is also able to develop our 'talent for speaking differently' about the already existing reality. It is my contention that Bauman helps us to confront the 'foreigners'' alternative cognitive frames while maintaining them as *untranslatable* languages. This is because he recognizes Rorty's assertion that we must develop our own vocabulary to describe what we understand as the quality of our own and others' understandings of the world. In this sense I want to argue that Bauman is the dragoman for sociology in liquid modern times.

THE DRAGOMAN OF SOCIOLOGY

Dragoman is a suitably resonant label for Bauman because he is the sociological hermeneutician *par excellence*. The term derives from the Arabic word *targuman* which literally means interpreter. As Bernard Lewis[14] argues, however, a dragoman is somebody who is more than just an interpreter; he is somebody who acts as a go-between, what Pierre Bourdieu has called in another context a cultural intermediary. The task of the dragoman is to establish a conversing tradition between one hermeneutic convention and another and at the same time make sure that the message from the one to the other is undistorted and clearly understood. This is what Bauman does in his sociology and this is what he is good at.

Bauman himself would be much too modest to make such bold claims for his own sociology, but in this chapter I shall argue that after decades of honourable service, sociology in its orthodox modern form could no longer be expected to yield the significance it once held and it was in the hands of Zygmunt Bauman that the sociologist's job, under such circumstances, was to reinvent the fundamental terms of its key reference points. In developing this critique, the chapter explores Bauman's special way of thinking sociologically and argues that it challenges the classical sociological orthodoxy by refusing to pursue the usual sociological template. And by the end, the reader should be able to grasp the key point that Bauman's work is not simply sociology: it has the full force of the sociological imagination within it. Indeed, Bauman's sociology is another rendition of C. Wright Mills's 'sociological imagination'[15] – both a meeting place between public issues and private troubles and a veritable remedy to awaken the sleeping sociologist in all of us. But as the discerning reader will see, in Bauman's hands, sociology is a cocktail that makes for a very special kind of brew, because in its paradigm-shifting endeavours it not only maintains the necessity of sociology but also at the same time questions sociology itself from a position which resists the endeavours of sociology to assign to it merely a sociological way of understanding the world.

As I pointed out in the introduction, Bauman is a sociologist who runs alone and has no particular sociological affiliations. What is perhaps his foremost merit and his most compelling contribution to sociology is the subtle way in which he challenges sociology's more established cognitive frames for looking at the world. As I also suggested in the introduction, Bauman has created his own particular style *and* substance for doing sociology, which is unique to him. Yet, as noted at the beginning of this chapter, Bauman has had very little to say about issues of methodology. So we need to explore the *orientation* of Bauman's sociology rather than what he himself has had to say about the ways and means of sociology in order to find the most compelling clues to what constitutes his own definitive sociological approach.

THE WAYS AND MEANS OF THE DRAGOMAN

Very much like the world he depicts in his books, Bauman's social thought is fractured, moving on various planes in different directions at once. There is the Bauman who is notoriously difficult to understand.[16] His sociology certainly has a particular flavour, which for students who are not familiar with it is frankly unappealing. This is because Bauman's sociology is of the old style. His writing style is restrained, exact, thoughtful, often lyrical, ironic, but most definitely not of the sound-bite. But it is a style which has the capacity to reflect the world as it is in itself. He is the essayist *par excellence* who can just as easily deliver a trilogy of books on a particular theme[17] as he can write a ground-breaking book on an issue as contentious as the Holocaust.

Then there is Bauman the man, who is much more accessible – living and working in Leeds, until 1990 professor of sociology at the city's university – and always open to an invitation to perform a lecture or seminar or do an interview. In his more recent work, Bauman, like Foucault before him, is increasingly coming to recognize that the interview format can communicate his ideas succinctly without losing any of their force or accuracy. However, the interviews, like the books and journal articles, are always precise affairs. Bauman prefers what Samuel Delaney[18] has called the 'silent interview', which recognizes that if the interviewer really wants to know what the interviewee *thinks* about certain matters, written interviews are more efficient than verbal exchanges.

There is also another Bauman, who has recently turned to pocket books – see for example, *Globalization: The Human Consequences* (1998), *Community: Seeking Security in an Insecure World* (2001), *Identity* (2004), and *Europe: An Unfinished Adventure* (2004) – which depict in their pages some of the most exacting accounts available of the most important social, cultural, political and economic changes affecting men and women's lives today. Indeed, Bauman's most recent books are a reflection of his increasing recognition that when all is said and done sociologists largely write for each other. As he might say, this is not merely because the majority of people have little interest in what sociologists say, but also because there is the little question of the thriving world of consumer culture to attend to. As a result Bauman is increasingly coming to recognize that if his sociology is to help the cause of human freedom it must speak to people in the ways which they appreciate; the majority of people are not interested in books about achieving freedom, they are interested in self-help books and lifestyle magazines. This is why Bauman's more recent writings are self-conscious hybrids comprising ready-made guides to living, full of astute sociological insights which go into a kind of existentialism his earlier more sociologically essayist books avoided, with the possible exception of *Mortality, Immortality and Other Life Strategies*.

As guide books to living, Bauman's more recent writings can also be seen as explicit attempts to render us more conscious of our individual freedom which is, at the current time, threatened by market forces and especially consumerism. In other words, Bauman wants us to speak to our destinies; he wants us to make our own wishes come true rather than have them made for us by consumer culture. Similar to Anthony Giddens,[19] it is also often the self-help manuals in the supplements of the Sunday newspapers to which Bauman turns in order to make his own guides to our lives and times, not particularly because they depict in their pages the most exacting accounts of the changes affecting men and women's lives today, but because they offer him some of the most cogent expressions of these processes which 'they chart out and help shape'.[20]

As Keith Tester[21] has observed, Bauman's writing over time reveals another kind of shift. As his ways of expressing his ideas have more and more turned to interviews and pocket books, he not only pays more attention to human relationships and their consequences, but he also pays less heed to precision in his use of concepts, to the extent that he appears to have an apparent disregard for terminological consistency. Perhaps this is because he now accepts that his responsibility is to supply guide books to living to liquid modern men and women who do not have time to read conventional social theory because they live their lives in such a hurry. This might be a problem if he were a lesser writer, but with Bauman it does not matter whether or not he demonstrates in his writings the specifics of every concept. This is because what Gabriel García Márquez once said of Franz Kafka is equally appropriate to Bauman: 'it is enough for him to have written it for something to be true, with no proof other than the power of his talent and the authority of his voice'.

This last point notwithstanding, I should like to argue that in his more recent writings Bauman has merely developed what the late Edward Said, and Adorno before him, called a 'late style' – a new idiom that great writers acquire towards the end of their lives which reflects the moment 'when the artist who is fully in command of his medium nevertheless abandons communication with the established social order of which he is a part and achieves a contradictory, alienated relationship with it'[22] – or what Bauman himself would no doubt call his ambivalent relationship with sociology. Bauman's work has not become in any way less rigorous; on the contrary, he just leaves out of his books what does not interest him. This not only leaves the reader with a sense of the enormity of the 'missing' work behind the work – which in turn gives his books the ambivalence of their 'substantial insubstantiality'[23] – but means that in adopting this 'late style' Bauman's sociology gets even more dazzlingly insightful, like the last minutes of a dying light bulb before it conks out.

In this regard, I want to argue that in his more recent writings there is a growing recognition that as the ever-more elaborate critical tools of sociology are now the new instruments of obfuscation, much sociological writing – including some of his own – is as unreadable as it is unread by the general public. As I pointed out above, Bauman's response to this has been to increasingly forgo his previously more essayist type sociology and revert to interviews and pocket books. This suggests that Bauman's is a sociology that is different in another sense, therefore, since it is able through its shape-shifting capacities to connect what are normally understood as disparate ways of thinking about the world to reveal for sociology something unfamiliar and surprising.

The point I want to make in the rest of this chapter is that Bauman merely has the gift of the sociological imagination, by which I mean he can create the world of the present instinctively without recourse to the theories and concepts of the old orthodox model or by acquiescing to the platitudes of the present. And the reason that he can see the present so clearly is because he has an equally convincing grasp of the past; when he is writing about liquid modernity he is at the same time showing an acute understanding of solid modernity, and it is this which gives his liquid modernity thesis such precision and critical cogency.

THE LITERARY BASIS OF BAUMAN'S SOCIOLOGY

Bauman is also like Giddens in the sense that he does not carry out primary empirical research in the manner of say a Bourdieu. In his work there are constant reminders that reality is much larger, more complex and various than any empirical work could hope to see. And if Bauman's sociology is an exemplary comment on the contemporary world which does not feel a need for local or forced empirical insights, it is one that is informed by a massive gathering of enjoyable erudition. What is significant about his approach is not so much a rejection of the techniques of empirical enquiry, although its rejection of the relentless pursuit of 'truth' marks a significant departure, rather it is the infusion of the sociological imagination with its literary basis that marks Bauman's sociology out. If his work is opposed to the dualism of 'theory' and 'empiricism' in sociology, it has more in common with the Kantian emphasis on the relationship between the 'empirical world' and 'creative spirit'. To this extent and in the words of that most astute social commentator, Roland Barthes, Bauman's sociology is guided 'not so much by reality as intelligibility'.

Some of Bauman's favourite novelists include Jorge Luis Borges, Milan Kundera, Italo Calvino and Georges Perec, and in his recent book on Bauman's social thought, Keith Tester has depicted Bauman as somebody who has the taste of a storyteller – a kind of sociological teller of tales who has created a sociology as a story all of his own which owes a great debt to the alternative ways of thinking about the world he has imported from these writers. But when Tester suggests that Bauman's sociology is 'possessed of a *literary edge*',[24] he does not go far enough; it is not sufficient to suggest that 'Bauman's sociology is a unique synthesis of literature filtered through ... critical theory'.[25] What these authors offer him are some of the most insistent themes that he pursues in his sociology.

In relation to what Bauman thinks about the pursuit of sociological knowledge, we can briefly consider the twin influences of Calvino and Borges on his work. From Calvino, Bauman recognizes the ambivalent status of sociology, as both a measure of the world and a denial of it. In an analogous way, from Borges he gleans the ability to erode the tenuous difference between 'fact' and 'fiction' in his sociology. But what Bauman has most learned from these authors is that in order that it should continue to have relevance, sociology needed another kind of understanding, so that it could be written successfully but only on quite different principles. Few sociologists writing today would care to defend the idea that there exists a separation between 'theory' work and 'empirical' work. In the practice of sociology, though, the old dichotomy lives on. But in his sociology Bauman realizes that empirical 'facts' on their own do not *persuade*, he recognizes too that 'theory' alone cannot *enlighten*; only by gaining an intimate connection with its literary basis can sociology achieve both those ends. Bauman's sociology is not the place to go to for 'facts' then, but it is instructive reading and what matters with his sociology is not so much the reality that underpins it, but the reality it creates for us, its readers.

But for all his use of literature Bauman is not a writer who is wrapped up in literary theory; his conviction of the importance of literature in enabling him to tell our truths much better than he could without it is what comes shining through in his work. The direction of his work is always to the meat and drink of everyday life; and if he remains loyal to his sociological roots it is not as a theoretician who loves to lose himself in ethereal obscurities, but as a poet for whom sociological analysis, however distinct it may be from what naïve empiricists call the real world, attempts to distil the meaning of the world to his readers. To this end, Bauman works with the quotidian like a potter at a wheel, spinning everyday life into ideas, concepts and theory that reflect the liquidity of the contemporary world in all its shape-shifting quality.

The challenge he sets himself is to employ these ideas, concepts and theories to help explain the truths of a liquid modernity – that time of permanent transition – in a way that clarifies this world. In Milan Kundera's fitting description, he projects on to the screen of sociology his own 'theatre of memory' which, when added to what it by now knows about the already existing reality, provides sociology with an alternative 'fantastic variation'.[26] In other words, Bauman uses sociology to replace reality rather than reproduce it; his sociology is a triumph of the socio-logical imagination over reality. In recognizing sociology's shadowing–boxing relationship with the world, Bauman offers an approach which, while recognizing the impossibility of sociology's ability to reproduce the world as it is, delivers its punches by making the invisible visible, by defamiliarizing the familiar.[27] In this sense it is the absence of limitations that is the mark of Bauman's project and in his writings he gives his readers the impression that anything is possible if sociologists dare to think it is. He might have a desire to understand the quotidian of the ordinary world simply 'as it is' but his aim is to redescribe it through the use of sociology, to endow that reality with the immense significance of its insignificance.

THE LIMITS OF CONVENTIONAL SOCIOLOGY

To read Bauman is to also recognize the shortcomings of other contemporary sociologists. One of the major problems with much of what is written in sociology today – particularly though not exclusively I'm talking about the sociology journals – is that it tends to be on the one hand heavily theoretical or on the other hand naively empiricist. In terms of the latter, this is evidenced in journal articles by the tendency towards methodological individualism and the predictable use of 'selected quotations' from 'key' respondents. Many of the sociologists who write this kind of stuff seem to work with the misconception that life as people say it is lived or life as it is lived is a fairly accurate representation of reality. The truth is that the sociologist must work with an acute awareness that what people say and do are often contradictory. People do not always act as they think and their actions for the most part do not correspond to what they feel, or even to what or whom they say they are, or what they intend. This is one of the key reasons why Bauman focuses on aesthetics – actions speak louder than words.

If for some in sociology, the meat and drink of their work must be grounded in the empirical, for others it has to be the kind of hard-edged conceptual stuff. Take for example Scott Lash,[28] who is as good a social theorist as they come, but who seems to pursue topical relevance at the expense of actually dealing with the indispensable human content that would give meaning to his packed esoteric concepts. He is the sociologist as social theorist, for whom the daily doings of everyday life are usurped by theory; therefore he tends to bypass the merely daily quotidian and go straight to the concepts, pure ideas, no flesh and blood expression. His sociology is simply too grand, too beyond the quotidian. In the end Lash, like so many other theory stalwarts around today, mistakes good sociological analysis for merely formulaic truths; and he may uncover a thousand different concepts in the pages but, in marked contrast to Bauman, he tells his readers very little about what it means to be human in our contemporary age.

Bauman, the sociologist as poet, achieves effects between the lines that are beyond the reach of both the social theorist and the empiricist. He might not seem to care at all about portraying social reality, yet it is obvious that what he paints portrays it far more accurately than any empiricist could even begin to imagine.

TOWARDS AN ANTI-ANTI RELATIVIST SOCIOLOGY

What I have suggested so far is that the opposition on which sociology finally runs aground – the one between 'theory' and 'method' – was inscribed within its *doxa* from the outset. As Bauman[29] points out, if orthodox sociology since its inception has been 'preoccupied with the conditions of obedience and conformity' and 'the opposition between conformity and deviance', its *modus operandi* for uncovering, demysti-fying and managing these 'problems' (at both an individual and societal level) is to this day too much rooted in the correspondence theory of truth. That is, the idea that the theories that sociologists develop about 'society' correspond with the 'facts'. This narrow empirical kind of sociology tends to switch between individuating and totalizing descrip-tions of the world 'out there', in the process making them equivalent in specificity to the imagined reality being addressed. As I pointed out in the introduction, what Bauman reminds us is that there is a contingency between what is 'real' and what is represented by sociologists in their writings.

Instead of arguing for truth as correspondence to some reality, then, Bauman, following Calvino and Borges, simply *makes* his own sociological truths as justification: warranted by his assertion that the *raison d'être* of sociology is to help the cause of human freedom. This doesn't stop Bauman from attempting to prise open the cracks between 'fact' and 'fiction', 'appearance' and 'reality', but what it does do is allow sociology to make an intimate connection with its literary basis in order to make its own truths without correspondence to the 'facts'. Culturally grounded conceptualization of truths, that prove themselves to be 'good in the way of belief, *and good, too, for definite, assignable reasons*',[30] ultimately helps us to see that the actually existing reality is much more complex than we once imagined.

By resisting the correspondence theory of truth in this way, Bauman, while still dealing with 'real' world issues, effectively dissolves the line between the theoretical and the empirical, between 'theory' and 'method' in sociology. By drawing on something like Rorty's strategy of redescription, Bauman shows his 'talent for speaking differently' about the ways and means of sociology, but, importantly, without surrendering to the relativism of postmodernism. As he points out, his position is best described as anti-anti relativistic[31] rather than relativistic, because

> [i]t is not true that all cultural values and precepts are equal just because of the fact that all of them have been chosen somewhere and at some stage of history. Some cultural solutions are indeed 'more equal than others' – though not in the once upheld sense of

being endemically superior answers to the universal problems of the human condition, but solely in the sense that unlike other cultures they are ready to consider their own historicity and contingency, and so also the possibility of comparison on equal terms. A culture [such as sociology] may claim superiority in so far as it is ready to look seriously at cultural alternatives [such as literature], treat them as partners for dialogue rather than passive recipients of monological homilies, and as a source of enrichment rather than collections of curios waiting to be censured, buried or confined to a museum. The superiority of such cultural solutions consists precisely in not taking its own substantive superiority for granted and acknowledging itself as a contingent presence, which like all contingent beings needs yet to justify itself in substantive terms – also in terms of its ethical value.

Bauman effectively collapses the distinction between realism and idealism to suggest that sure enough there is a 'real', material world 'out there', but we can only know that world through the contingency of our own redescriptions of it, which can be found in all manner of descriptions, images and metaphors.

From the above discussion we can also discern that ethical issues are central to Bauman's project. However, what differentiates Bauman's sociology is that it does not rely on universally accepted canons and formalized institutions for debate, it accepts that ' "a never ending conversation" is played out in the arena of culture, where humankind has created its own polity, "little by little", through ever larger and richer "compounds of opposed values" '.[32] Adopting Bauman's position for the sociology then does not mean accepting that 'anything goes'. On the contrary, it means that without the obligation of having to make their work take on an essentialist position, sociologists can get on with the task of constructing their own narratives about the actually existing reality. For Bauman, as for Rorty, ethical questions must be dealt with in the untidy realm of human interaction rather than in the tidy transcendental realm of universal reason. And it is precisely because the sociologist is now in a stronger position to recognize and make explicit the ideological, subjective, and fictive elements in their writings that our understanding of the already existing reality can be advanced. Bauman recognizes that the challenge for sociology is to construct narratives that work, but which do not claim rights to *the* truth in the essentialist sense; in Rorty's words, *real theories* that are 'true enough', but which recognize 'that there will never be a final resting-place for thought'.[33] Indeed, contrary to the postulations of some,[34] Bauman's sociology always refutes the 'legislative moment', as it recognizes that there is always something more that can be said.

Bauman's sociology effectively pushes for a hermeneutically driven analysis that steers a course between the Scylla of postmodernism and the Charybdis of sociology that is still 'nineteenth-centuryish'.[35] It excels not in relativism but in the particularity of its exploration of the complex detail of human lives. However, if his sociology stands for the belief that the already existing reality exists, it does so in the knowledge that sociology's ability to know that reality is fated to remain incomplete, because every sociology, no matter how assiduously researched, is bound to be irredeemably ignorant of some matters. Bauman's sociology suggests that what we all need to recognize is that what we learn about the already existing reality from sociology books is only a domesticated version of the 'real' thing. Real life is as unpredictable as it is contingent, fragmented and uncertain.

In the light of these observations and in the words of that most perceptive of commentators, Jacques Derrida, what Bauman sets out to achieve in his work is a kind of sociology that will 'deck itself out in "realism" just in time to fall short of the thing'.[36] To paraphrase Joseph Natoli, this is the kind of sociology that goes on without the baggage of pretending to have a universal rule of judgement and justification; it wastes no time creating and defending so-called rigorous, objective, analytical methodologies, just as it wastes no time in pretending it is employing a universal, absolute Reason or any system of logic based on an independent critical reason.[37]

Yet despite their obvious lack of empirical detail, Bauman's books are always prompted by life as it is lived: something seen, something heard. Their narrative threads come from elsewhere, too: from his thoughts, interests and preoccupations. With Bauman we are rather nudged into a fresh way of thinking sociologically about the world we inhabit. And the result is more compelling than any empirical study could offer. Yet developing this kind of sociology means that Bauman is not only content to not know everything about the already existing reality, but that he is also in a strong position to dwell on issues of ambivalence and contingency.

HERMENEUTIC SOCIOLOGY AND SOCIOLOGICAL HERMENEUTICS

Every sociological book or article embodies an epistemological decision, an interpretation of how and what its author perceives, which means that the actually existing realities sociologists talk about in their writings have no meaning without interpretation, without hermeneutics. Hermeneutics derives from textual interpretation in biblical studies, but its modern counterpart is secular in inspiration. Heidegger's more modern understanding distinguishes the practice of hermeneutics as an interpretative mode of 'being-in-the world' which the hermeneutician orients himself to. In Bauman's hands, the hermeneutic 'method' is artistic and represents a clear challenge to the dominant vision of the 'natural science of the social',[38] not merely because it is concerned with the intuitive interpretation of the 'structure of feeling' in Raymond Williams's sense,[39] as opposed to focusing its critical gaze on the cause and effect of positivistic regularities, but also because it 'emphasises that actions, events and social processes must be understood and interpreted from the standpoint of their subjective meaning for the actors under consideration and from the standpoint of their specific historical and cultural context'.[40] Bauman's is a mode of hermeneutic inquiry that is thoroughly self-absorbed and his autobiography intrudes throughout. As Bauman himself makes plain, there could be no other way with sociology 'made to the measure' of liquid modernity: 'There is no choice between "engaged" or "neutral" ways of doing sociology. A non-committal sociology is an impossibility.'[41]

The argument implied by the practice of hermeneutic sociology has a clear affinity with Lyotard's focus on the idea of truth as style and performativity. It reminds us not that reality is socially constructed by sociologists, and not even that sociologists simply tell stories, but that life can be told by sociologists as it is actually lived, and rather extravagantly told at that. This hermeneutic kind of looking is about watching, smelling, studying, listening, above all else imagining, viscerally; and the combination of an involved but at the same time ironic distancing in the act of seeing. This research approach requires the sociologist to literally go out of his own mind, shed for the time being his own sense of self, and enter the world that he is researching – become part of that world, think how the 'locals' think and adopt the points of view and narrative voices different from his own; sense the trajectory of that experience of the world, which entails knowing the influences that move it.

This hermeneutic way of doing intellectual work also makes the tacit assumption that there is no single understanding of reality and that there is no observation that is not discursively positioned. It assumes that every understanding and observation is theory-laden. It also recognizes its own limitations. The strength of interpretive intellectual work lies in its ability to be 'up front' about its own weaknesses and in its sensitivity to the practical contingencies involved in 'doing' analyses of the local cultural variety. In this sense, Bauman's recognition about the limitations of the empirical paradoxically confirms the prestige of realism in sociology, its true rigour and challenge.

For Bauman, hermeneutic or interpretive intellectual work functions as a corrective to the detached deployment of modern, authoritative legislative reason. Contrary to legislative reason, interpretive intellectual work implies both a commitment and an attachment of the subject in the object, made manifest by what Charles Taylor calls a 'perspicuous articulation',[42] rather than a relation of correspondence between the object and some 'outside' account. For Taylor, perspicuous articulation can only be achieved through a form of knowing that relates to that of a hermeneutic conversation – there is no epistemological split in the interpretive scheme of things – which is invariably locally situated.

For Bauman, legislative reason objectifies, not only rationally but also ontologically and ethically. However, in the point of view of interpretive intellectual work there is the recognition that no object is simply an object of knowledge. Where the legislator gazes at his object as something that cannot return his look, the interpreter recognizes that the fusion between himself and the thing that he is surveying is everything. With interpretive work the thing which seduces the intellectual does so through its look, by suggesting it might just be interesting if he is prepared to develop a deeper understanding of its special ontological power. In fact, to fulfil his interpretive role of facilitating difference – by extending communication between autonomous communities – the interpreter must develop a deep understanding in order 'to maintain the delicate balance between … conversing traditions … for the message to be undistorted (regarding the meaning of the sender) and understood (by the recipient)'.[43]

In Rorty's meaning, interpretive intellectual work aims to deconstruct the 'privileged position' of legislative reason to 'change the subject' to an alternative vocabulary, that is an 'abnormal discourse', which does not oblige the interpreter to have to make her work take on the 'normal discourse' of legislative reason, which tends to preclude alternative ways of social inquiry. Interpretive intellectual work not only translates ideas between different interpretive communities, then, it makes meaning. However, as Bauman[44] points out, the interpreter does not attempt to justify that meaning in the rationalist, legislative sense, by spelling out beforehand the criteria or methodology by which her work should be assessed. The interpreter reasons that her work will have to succeed on the basis of its own merits; it will have to have relevance for other interpreters. It will work for different people and in different ways.

Bauman's understanding of hermeneutics also deconstructs the false dichotomy between subject and object,[45] between surface and depth in social inquiry with its insistence on undecidability. For Bauman,[46] concepts are like human beings; they are not simply good or bad but hold both and other possibilities. This is why he can bracket together theorists as diverse as Hans Gadamer and Richard Rorty as hermeneutic interpreters, because each of these theorists grasps what is required of an adequate mode of intellectual inquiry for liquid modern times. The fact that Gadamer organizes his hermeneutic intellectual work in a deep sense, while Rorty, in company with Foucault, subordinates deep hermeneutics to surface hermeneutics, is neither here nor there. For Bauman, these alternative positions are commensurable in the sense that each offers a kind of post-scientific way of understanding the world – best understood as a hermeneutics of cultural orientation – which has established its superiority over legislating modes of inquiry.

MAKING HERMENEUTICS SOCIOLOGICAL

Above, I suggested that Bauman is a dragoman and that what he does in his sociology is set himself the task of establishing conversing traditions between different hermeneutic conventions. That hermeneutics has its own literary basis in that it derives from the interpretation of texts is not lost on Bauman, but what he tries to do in his work is make hermeneutics more sociological and so doing he suggests that there are two kinds of hermeneutics available to sociologists in the pursuit of their vocation: hermeneutic sociology and sociological hermeneutics. In a recent interview with Bauman,[47] I asked him to differentiate between the two. As he put it:

> hermeneutic sociology seems to me but one way among many good ways of doing a sociological job, while sociological hermeneutics (i.e. decoding the meaning of human actions in reference to social conditions) seems to be the job all sociology true to its vocation is bound to perform. This is at any rate what I try, however ineptly, to do all along. I attempt to make trends in human conduct and beliefs intelligible as collective results of the lay efforts to make sense of the socially produced conditions and to devise appropriate life strategies. You may say that making hermeneutics *sociological* is one more name for 'sociological imagination'. In my view, the two concepts should become in sociological practice coextensive.

In Bauman's sense, to interpret is in effect an attempt to paraphrase the already existing reality, in order to make something corresponding to it, but something that does not claim to be the definitive truth in the essentialist meaning. As the above quote from Bauman implies, hermeneutic sociology attempts to understand life and in so doing it tries to elucidate not only the consciousness and unconsciousness of individual social actors, but the quotidian as it is experienced, just then, at that moment, as and when it occurs, before the corrections and distortions that sociology inevitably imposes. As Bauman himself puts it, the hermeneutic sociologist

> is one who, securely embedded in his own, 'native' tradition, penetrates deeply into successive layers of meanings upheld by the relatively alien tradition to be investigated. The process of penetration is simultaneously that of translation. In the person of the sociologist, two or more traditions are brought into communicative contact – and thus open up to each other their respective contents which otherwise would remain opaque. The [hermeneutic] sociologist aims at 'giving voice' to cultures which without his help would remain numb or stay inaudible to the partner in communication. [The hermeneutic] sociologist operates at the interface between 'language games' or 'forms of life'. His mediating activity is hoped to enrich both sides of the interface.[48]

The hermeneutic sociologist communicates the culture of the form of life in a way that allows it to 'reveal itself' to the reader, to represent the 'self-evidential reality' of the world it reflects. Essentially, the way hermeneutic sociology is written can be seen as an attempt to extend the reach of the 'form of life' in question to readers who are not familiar with such a world in order to illuminate that world for them in all its ambivalent complexity.

Hermeneutic sociology

Hermeneutic sociology not only recognizes and celebrates the subjectivity of the research process, but it also understands that what we know intuitively remains beyond what we can possibly 'discover' empirically. It recognizes too that the sociological knowledge it makes is also intuitively created through a kind of 'knowable community'.[49] For Williams, any knowable community has got to be approached in terms of its authors' viewpoints and consciousness. In my own book, *Leisure Life*,[50] I developed a hermeneutic sociological approach to make knowable the leisure life-world of a group of men who I called 'the lads'. The book focused its attention on a social network of a group of working-class men with whom I had grown up. In carrying out the research for the book, I realized that what I was exploring was a leisure life-world I had shared with some of my life-long friends and acquaintances, with whom I had shared so much. This also meant that the study would be about their leisure life-world, my leisure life-world, our leisure life-world.

Accordingly, I argued that this leisure life-world was characterized by a mutually engaged responsiveness between me and the rest of 'the lads' which united us through our shared knowledge. And in one stroke I was also able to deconstruct the opposition between involvement and detachment in the research process. I suggested that:

> The discourse of the leisure life-world has its own lexicon and we, 'the lads', read from our mutual discourse. When we are together conversation moves from subject to subject, moving one way and then the other. We can finish each other's sentences, and communicate, more remarkably, without speaking at all. With a real affinity, and in the spirit of the communion that exists between each of us, we also use gestures known only to ourselves. For when we are at our leisure, we are one. I know 'the lads' and they know me: the relationship between the knower and the known in the research process is therefore an intimate one.[51]

I went on to argue that this leisure life-world could only be interpreted by the reader of the book through my way of seeing. Following Bauman, I argued that the leisure life-world of 'the lads' was a postulated community and that what was required for exploring this 'home' 'stripped of all material features' was a kind of hermeneutic sociology. In this way, the book dealt with the problem of confronting the actually existing reality of 'the lads' head on, by exposing the limitations of conventional ethnography. It was suggested that it was not enough to research a social phenomenon such as the leisure life-world directly the way to both approach and 'reveal' its otherworldliness was through the tactics of hermeneutics, a kind of mimesis for representing this actually existing reality, but which did so uncompromisingly through a dialectics of ethnography and intuition, invoked through pragmatism. In the words of Henning Bech, this hermeneutic approach worked because it was able to 'snuggle up to what [was] quotidian and recognizable, even trivial, for the inhabitants of the life-world'.[52]

Henning Bech is a sociologist whose work Bauman greatly admires, and especially his book *When Men Meet: Homsexuality and Modernity*, which he considers to be an 'exemplary exercise in reaching the totality through a case study'.[53] Bauman recognizes that there are few sociologists with Bech's ability to practise hermeneutic sociology. This is because hermeneutic sociology is a craft which requires not only the appropriate post-scientific cultural 'sociological imagination' (or what Bauman sometimes calls the sociological sixth sense), but also the ability to write in the kind of poetic language or 'talent for speaking differently', which

Rorty calls 'redescription'. Indeed, what hermeneutic sociologists such as Bech are good at is elucidating the actually existing reality as it is seen by the 'locals' in ways that speak in the language of the 'locals' – as we saw above by elucidating what Rorty calls 'foreigners'' alternative cognitive frames.

According to Bauman, however, if this aspect is the major strength of hermeneutic sociology it is also the source of its major weakness. As Peter Nijhoff[54] puts it, hermeneutic sociology 'is expressly limited to explicating the interpretations [of any given totality], as effective in the field under study – it will not attempt to explain them in any way'. In the final analysis, just as Blackshaw's leisure life-world is restricted to explicating the lives and times of 'the lads' in a discourse which embraces those lives and times in their own terms of reference, so Bech's hermeneutics is restricted to the discourse of gay men and cultures of homosexuality.

SOCIOLOGICAL HERMENEUTICS

As Nijhoff goes on to point out, sociological hermeneutics on the other hand, 'constantly moves back and forth between explicating social constructs and explaining them'. Sociological hermeneutics goes beyond hermeneutic sociology in the sense that it seeks to establish a conversing tradition between two or more different hermeneutic traditions rather than restricting itself to elucidating one particular life-world. In other words, sociological hermeneutics is dragoman interpretation because it recognizes the 'need to maintain the delicate balance between the two conversing traditions necessary for the message to be undistorted (regarding the meaning invested by the sender) and understood (by the recipient)'.[55] The practice of sociological hermeneutics

> consists, in a nutshell, in reading the observed behavioural tendencies against the conditions under which actors find themselves obliged to go about their life-tasks. The tendencies in question can be seen as the sediments of the search for adequacy – but though the actors do their best to act reasonably, their actions are all too often off the targets that could secure the adequacy, targets that stay essentially out of the actors' reach and so render 'really existing' adequacy permanently wanting.[56]

What Bauman is here suggesting is that if the key role of sociology is to help the cause of human freedom it has to deal with the issue that many individuals and communities, but especially poor and oppressed groups, are prevented from experiencing the same freedoms which are open to other more fortunate individuals and communities. He is also suggesting that the correspondence between what individual social actors think they do and what they actually do is often out of sync, to the extent that they are, as Rorty would say, 'more or less out of touch' with the implications of what the actually existing reality means for their individual freedom. As the reader will see in the final chapter of this book, Bauman suggests that it is through analysing the impact of consumer culture on the lives of individuals and communities that we can see why many people are more or less out of touch with their realities.

OSTRANENIE, METAPHOR AND SOCIOLOGICAL HERMENEUTICS

As Keith Tester has argued, Bauman's sociology is inspired by Gramsci's understanding of the world as the product of praxis, which inspires his sociology to seek 'to demonstrate that the world "does not have to be like this", that "there is an alternative" '.[57] In this way, Bauman challenges what has essentially become the domestication of the orthodox sociological template, because his work tries to not only make sense of the world, but also find as yet 'hidden' possibilities for change. In emphasizing its commitment to praxis, Bauman's sociology signifies a refusal to be constrained within the limits of familiarity or 'how things seem to be'.[58] As Bauman has suggested

Familiarity is the staunchest enemy of inquisitiveness and criticism … [and in] encounter with [the] familiar world ruled by habits and reciprocally reasserting beliefs, sociology acts as a meddlesome and often irritating stranger. It disturbs the comfortingly quiet life by asking questions no one among the 'locals' remembers being asked, let alone answered. Such questions make evident things into puzzles: they defamiliarize the familiar. Suddenly, the daily way of life must come under scrutiny. It now appears to be just one of the possible ways, not the one and only, not the 'natural', way of life.[59]

In defamiliarizing the familiar the sociologist enters another world, both stranger and more revealing than the one he thinks he already knows.

As we have seen already, despite their obvious lack of empirical detail, Bauman's books are always prompted by life as it is lived: something seen, something heard. We have seen that the narrative threads of his writing come from elsewhere, too: from his thoughts, interests and preoccupations. With Bauman we are in effect nudged into a fresh way of thinking sociologically about the world we inhabit through the poetic manoeuvre of ostranenie, 'to produce a semantic shift which makes the habitual appear strangely unfamiliar, rather than as though it were being perceived for the first time.'[60] And as I have already argued the result is more compelling than any empirical study could ever offer. Indeed, Bauman's sociology unashamedly confronts the void left in the pursuit of empirical 'data' by interpolating passages of everyday life with the personal input of the sociologist. It is atmosphere that is crucial to his work and what brings it atmosphere is metaphor.

Metaphor is the rhetorical tool which Bauman uses to enable him to defamiliarize the familiar and show it in a new light. And it is to hermeneutics that Bauman turns in order to develop his own conversing tradition of ostranenie. In other words, he recognizes that metaphor is that part of language that allows him to do hermeneutics. And it is to metaphors and the metaphoric process rather than merely analogy that Bauman turns in order to maximize his own 'talent for speaking differently' about the worlds he makes in his sociology.[61] Bauman takes Rorty to his world when he recognizes that metaphoricity is of vital importance for developing new ways of seeing in sociology, by providing the basis for 'new language games' in Lyotard's meaning.

As we have seen, Bauman's is a version of sociological hermeneutics that is a politically and morally inspired critique which argues for a plural world in which nobody is shut out or excluded. What is more, like Marx, he *thinks* as a man of *action*.[62] Accordingly the aim of his sociology is always to stress the realness of the already existing reality. This is not to say that he is a realist in the classic philosophical meaning, but to emphasize that his sociology is written with the same social and political venom found in the writings of the great English novelist and journalist George Orwell. Bauman's work prods at the sorest, most critical problems facing the human condition. He is a writer who has the capacity to not only demonstrate to his readers the poverty, repression, exclusion and violence perpetuated against those at the margins of liquid modernity but also to show them how these conditions arise and most crucially how they are linked to their own comfortable existences.

Bauman recognizes that metaphors are useful tools in writing sociology because in their stubborn explicitness they force the reader to interpret them, which he knows, of course, is part of the hermeneutician's job. In particular, he uses these metaphorical settings to illustrate the points where obduracy meets restless liquidity in a compelling way to explore the tensions and ambivalence between our yearning for a stable world and our stubborn insistence on change. In Bauman's hands, metaphors become much more than simply explanatory devices, however, as they provide him with a means for giving voices to the socially excluded. When

Bauman talks about the denizens of liquid modernity he sees himself as a denizen rather than merely an observer of denizens; he associates with the outcasts and the forgotten of liquid modernity.

Bauman acknowledges that his own grimy lexicon of metaphors owes much to Mary Douglas's work in *Purity and Danger*,[63] and he always lays them on thick and fast like rockets in order to elucidate meaning in his writing and seldom do they miss their intended targets. Following Douglas, Bauman shows how strangers tend to be constructed through the idea of pollution or dirt.[64] Dirt in the cultural sense is not something that is inherently 'dirty', but something that is applied to strangers who take on the appearance of 'dirtiness' in situations where they do not fit, do not belong. Dirt in Douglas's sense is therefore an effect of a socially constructed system of classification, a culturally defined symbolic mapping of what belongs where. Through this system of classification, dirt is constructed as a foreign body, a pollutant which should be kept in its own habitat. It does not have a place in 'our' symbolic mapping of what belongs where because it disrupts our system of classification through its 'otherness'.

It is through metaphor that Bauman[65] brings our attention to the modern appeal of the idea of the viscous (*le visqueux*) as an existential category which both at once alarms and fascinates us. This is a concept Bauman borrows from Sartre and he suggests it is one of the key existential categories through which modern men and women make sense of their whole mode of being-in-the-world. The metaphor of *le visqueux* invokes a whole range of possible manifestations and which ultimately is its appeal; it serves as an ambivalent image that both at once *threatens* the modern consciousness (which as Bauman shows is a completing and ordering appropriation of the world) and *fascinates* it because it appears as a stranger or an alien, an unmelting presence refusing and simply deemed unable to play by local rules. Bauman puts particular emphasis on the 'slimy' character of *le visqueux*, which is just one of a range of its possible manifestations. As we saw in the last chapter, in *Modernity and the Holocaust*, Bauman demonstrated how the Jew was constructed as the living embodiment of *le visqueux,* an amalgam of all that was unwelcome, abnormal and detestable in Nazi Germany.

It is through these kinds of metaphors that Bauman transforms sociology from a medium through which sociologists largely read and write for each other, into a political and ethical forum for witnessing the unsettling – sociology as a kind of willed engagement with Otherness. There is no denying that Bauman's writing has some of the force of poetry in the subtlety in which he makes images through metaphors, which in their power and recurrences are meant to unsettle his readers – he forces them to absorb the noxious smells of the world that surrounds them, but which they choose to turn their backs on. For example, in *Wasted Lives: Modernity and its Outcasts*, it is through the use of metaphor that Bauman captures both the smell and the scale of the poverty and inequality associated with social exclusion in a liquid modern world that he argues is to all intents and purposes full. Bauman's account of these 'wasted lives' has a buzzing immediacy which is both magnificent and heartbreaking, without ever being sentimental and here he lays bare liquid modernity's tangled, toxic roots. According to Bauman, waste is the oozing sore of liquid modernity and it is set among those whose existence we mostly prefer not to think about, the outcasts – those zombie characters without jobs or homes. In this work, Bauman not only discusses the human cost of the macro political machinations involved, but also the ways in which countries in the western world paint their worries onto the increasing influx of asylum seekers they find at their ports, and in the process freeze-frame them in a picture of 'dirty' Otherness.

As we saw in the last chapter, in common with Max Weber's sociological approach, Bauman also practises 'ideal-typical' analysis, but not in a way like the empty proceduralism found in the pages of the sociology journals. Of the range of means Bauman possesses for giving himself something to say, one of the most effective is his aphorist's ability to evoke dualities: solid modern and liquid modern, parvenu and pariah, tourist and vagabond.

A good example of this type of analysis is once again *Wasted Lives*, where Bauman compares the fates of the outcasts – who, reminiscent of the refugee Karl Rossman in Kafka's *Amerika*, are obliged to keep on producing their identification papers and have to live with the constant fear of deportation on the margins of society – with those more affluent members of the liquid modernity, the 'tourists' and the 'players', who, safe in the knowledge that their passports allow them to pass through any port of call, can travel around the world seemingly at will. For Bauman, the lives of the better-off in the globalized world can be understood through metaphors such as these because they have the means to freely wander around the world, while the outcasts as the 'vagabonds' they are imagined to be are forced to wander because of the 'scarcity of settled places'.[66] In this way, Bauman is able to not only illustrate divisions in mobility, but also emphasize to his readers the limits these categories of living place on individual freedom.

Bauman's writing here is intuitive as it shows the horror of the dark underbelly of capitalism in the liquid modern age. The effects of those lives lived as human waste come reeling off the pages, forcing the reader to think the unthinkable, and the writing leaves the reader as it intends –

both breathless and bruised. Nothing in sociology comes more visceral than this, short of the actual physical involvement. And if we don't want to see the terrible consequences of modernity in lives of others less fortunate than ourselves, we are made to feel it through Bauman's sociology. Through the blizzards of metaphors he forces us to do what we cannot do in real life – enter the world of the Other. He uses the rage of the storm to shout at his readers, as it were: 'look at the plight of these people and recognize your own conspiracy in their fates!' In this way, he alerts us to the sickness inherent in our own culture of excessive consumption which we enjoy at the same time as we are busying ourselves erecting walls to keep out those who are fleeing poverty, war and persecution. Bauman tries to make you think about the exclusion of others, those terrible dehumanized experiences and degrading images of refugees, shuffling humiliated from one nowhere-ville to the next: people treated as objects.

SOCIOLOGY AS RESPONSIBILITY

Bauman also turns to the theme of responsibility more explicitly in his brief discussion of the ways and means of sociology in the essay 'Afterthought: On Writing; On Writing Sociology' at the end of *Liquid Modernity*. Here he criticizes orthodox sociology on the basis that its *doxa* was made on the premise of the opposition between conformity and deviance, which, as Bauman points out, merely mimed the reifying habits of the structural functionalist approach through which it was developed. As Bauman shows, this is evidenced in orthodox sociology's obsession with the circumstances of human conformity and obedience, which meant that if it allowed the ideas of 'deviant' and 'abnormal' to emerge as unexceptional, it was also unquestioning of its own role in finding for modern society the most efficient means to normalize 'deviance' and 'abnormality'.

As Bauman well knows, after the 1960s there emerged a range of theoretical strands which gave sociology the conflict perspective it initially lacked, resisting in the process structural functionalism's remorseless abstraction of human experience. What unified what was essentially a fast-emerging alternative sociology of theoretically divergent perspectives, was its collective willingness to 'side with the underdog'. Indeed, there was no logical reason why structural Marxists should necessarily concern themselves with developments in the anti-structuralist interests of symbolic interactionism, yet such interchanges became characteristic of conflict sociology. But the problem with this counter *doxa* was that it merely replaced the opposition between conformity and deviance with the opposition between 'truth' and 'illusion'.

As we have seen throughout this and the last chapter, this dichotomy is problematic for Bauman who not only takes phenomenology at its word by dispensing with questions about 'appearance' and 'reality', 'illusion' and 'truth', but who follows Rorty's lead in recognizing that deconstruction should not stop us making *our* own worlds in our own sociologies. As I pointed out in the preface of this book, we should simply remember that the worlds we make are *our* own worlds which we cannot claim to represent *the* world as it is in itself. In other words, we must use our 'talent for speaking differently' about the world in ways that are able to describe what we understand as the quality of our own understandings of the actually existing reality.

Bauman also shows us that when we make our *own* realities about the world in our sociologies, we must be prepared to admit that they will always be contested and tempered by contingency. To this extent he recognizes that the fundamental lesson of Marxism for sociology is that we must always be aware that *every* position is unavoidably ideological – sociologists, like anybody else, cannot be immunized against developing their own ideologies. Bauman's alternative kind of sociology suggests that if we want to argue convincingly for our way of understanding the world, we must recognize that we cannot resort to any foundational criteria for justifying that our version of that world is better than anybody else's, and all we can do is simply try to describe our sociologies in ways that are convincing, that work. In marked contrast to Marxism, then, Bauman does not see the world 'out there' as a battle between good (Marxism) and evil (capitalism), such as a war against ambivalence; good and evil can exist anywhere. As a result the choice for sociology is not one of taking sides but between responsibility and taking shelter from responsibility.

SOME CONCLUDING REMARKS ON THE RESPONSIBILITIES OF SOCIOLOGY, OF SOCIOLOGISTS

The truth is that there is no certain way of telling the real from the feigned, the actual from the imitation, and accordingly Bauman suggests that the challenge facing sociology today is not about uncovering the 'truth' behind the 'illusion' but about the opposition between *responsibility* and *bystanding*. He redescribes sociology as a matter of choice between taking individual *responsibility* for what we say and do in our sociologies or *bystanding* and 'taking shelter where responsibility for one's action need not be taken by the actors'.[67] For sociology, as for the quotidian, Bauman is appealing to the possibilities of a social transformation of the kind envisaged by the philosopher Emmanuel Levinas in which the relationship between self and Other is coextensive and marked by an incalculable mutual responsibility which begins with my recognition of his or her subjectivity.[68]

So instead of offering any ready-made guidelines for doing sociology, Bauman merely offers an orientation, with strong ethical and political undercurrents, which, if it cannot base its truths on foundational criteria, can resolve itself to try to be always *responsible* for the Other. In this sense, what Bauman is offering us is a way of doing sociology which is an indictment of those *bystanders* whose actions and complicity perpetuate oppression and exploitation in order to limit human freedom. It is also a kind of sociology which demands a never-ending hermeneutic dialogue between those who promulgate *seemingly* the most irreconcilable interpretations of the actually existing reality, as well as a constant questioning of ourselves and the institutions that surround us and, just as importantly, our own tacitly accepted assumptions about the world we make in our own sociologies.

4

Freedom and Security in the Liquid Modern Sociality

> There are two 'meta-values' undersigning human pursuits: freedom and security. One without the other is hell – but no attempt to balance one against the other has been so far found to be made in paradise's likeness. We go on trying …
>
> Zygmunt Bauman[1]

How close can sociologists really get to quotidian lives of ordinary men and women in a world in which 'our life struggles dissolve … in [an] *unbearable lightness of being*' – a time 'when we never know for sure when to laugh and when to cry. And there is hardly a moment in life to say without dark premonitions: "I have arrived".'[2] Can we really know what ordinary men and women reason, and think, and argue about when going through the course of daily lives which are fragmented, insecure and teeming with ambivalence? Is it possible for us to project onto the pages of our books their private worlds, their dreams and what goes on inside their heads? These are the kinds of questions that over the last ten years have increasingly come to concern Zygmunt Bauman, and during that time led him to produce a kind of sociology that more intimately than any other has the ability to take us right there into the mish-mash of this present predicament, into the soft melt that is liquid modernity.

'The job of sociology is to study "society", while it is the job of psychology to deal with individual behaviour', or so we have been led to believe. Indeed, sociology and psychology as we have come to know them in the modern university system, developed along these parallel lines. But as suggested in the last chapter, Bauman does not pay any attention to extant academic boundaries in his work and in this chapter I want to argue that what he offers us is a kind of *Bildungsroman*[3] sociology which merges psychology – or more precisely psychoanalysis – with phenomenology through hermeneutics, specifically because they are each concerned with interpretation. That psychoanalysis is conventionally understood as being concerned with the unconscious and phenomenology with the conscious is neither here nor there for Bauman; it is their combined efficacy for sociology that counts – as we have seen throughout this book, one of the key developments in his work is to do away with the dualisms which continue to hinder sociological thinking.

Freud is the master of unconscious desire and psychological ambivalence and Bauman captures the best he can offer the sociological imagination. Having said that, the reader should also note that if Bauman's sociology is psychoanalytical it is existentially so, and differs from the Freudian variety in being less deterministic and not in any shape or form scientific.[4] Existentialism is a type of philosophical thinking – rather than a movement as such – which takes existence to be that which is assumed though the experience of 'being-in-the-world'. Bauman is of an age to have seen existentialism come and go, replaced by poststructuralism and postmodernism, but it is its stress on the ideas of personal responsibility and choice and the demands these make on individual lives that are freely chosen that interests him. To this extent, Bauman's interest in existentialism shares much in common with that of Jean-Paul Sartre, who as Karl Simms points out, imported the material theory of Marx into existentialism, and in so doing took it in an atheist direction, which suggested that 'being-in-the-world' is 'not between existence and eternity, but between existence and nothing'.[5] In this sense, Sartre was one of the first philosophers to really grasp the point of the central conflict that underpins modern lives: the subjective centrality of men and women's own individuality versus the awareness of their own insignificance.

For Bauman, as for Sartre, the individual liberated through reflexivity is not so much rational as burdened with choice, and is at every turn faced with the need to make decisions; it is up to the individual to choose the life he or she thinks is best. Indeed, Bauman emerges in this chapter closer to Sartre than to Freud because the former insists on a kind of existential psychoanalysis which maintains that life is contingent and people are utterly contingent beings: if individuals choose to live their lives in particular ways, things could always be different.[6] In this regard it is not at all surprising too to see Bauman replacing Giddens's idea of *ontological insecurity*[7] with that of *existential insecurity* in sociology, because his work is alive to the existential in-between dilemmas facing men and women in their everyday lives today: for example, young Bradford-born Muslim women torn between the connections they have with Western popular culture and a lifetime of tradition and respect for their parents' wishes; young London-born Afro-Caribbean men whose patois, in between mobile phone calls, zips between cockney rhyming slang and Jamaican roots. In this sense, Bauman demonstrates that individuals in liquid modernity have to be a miasma of competing selves: parental, sexual, and political and everything else, and that sociology like no other academic discipline has the ability to offer something to those individuals 'keenly seeking wisdom they can use when struggling, alone and on their own, using their own skills and wits, with their life tasks, with relating to other people, with tying together the otherwise absent bonds and holding the partnerships they desire to last or breaking free from commitments they find constraining'.[8]

For Bauman, as for Sartre, liquid moderns are the masters of their own fates who make their own choices. However, if Sartre's 'ideal' reflective actors were those individuals *de facto* who, like artists, are able to create their identities as their own works of art, according to no pre-existing models,[9] Bauman's 'actual' reflective actors remain, on the whole, merely individuals *de jure*, who by and large create their own DIY models from those already pre-fabricated in consumer culture. As the reader will see in the following pages, what Bauman is suggesting is that liquid moderns are all too ready to absorb their ideas ready-made, which has implications for a number of aspects of their lives, but most notably when life does not work for them, when they tend to be inclined to blame the manufacturers rather than taking responsibility for it themselves. What Bauman suggests is the major upshot of this is that liquid modern identities are more likely than not bound to remain merely surfaces because they are never entirely their own.

The reader will also see that whereas Sartre always articulated in his existentialism a compelling sense of the angst facing men and women in their day-to-day existences, Bauman seems more interested in articulating the sheer energy of liquid modern lives which for all their self-imposed troubles are made by men and women who are too busy expanding the possibilities of their horizons ever to be too worried about the deepening psychological drama this brings to themselves and others they encounter in developing the life strategies which on the one hand pull them together and on the other drive them apart.

FREEDOM AND SECURITY

The issues relating to freedom and security cling to Bauman's analyses like chewing gum to a shoe and although he is certainly not the first sociologist to explore their competing claims on individual lives, the reader will see that in his work it is the supremacy of the individual self – self-identity, self-reliance, self-reference and self-transcendence – which emerges as the pivotal importance between the two, because he recognizes that liquid modern men and women are first and foremost individuals who are always guided by themselves rather than by the will of others. According to Bauman, DIY individual identity seeking is our fate in liquid modernity and our every action takes on the imprint of individuali-zation. This is a tall order for any one individual and it is no wonder that we spend a good deal of our time trying to find some breathing space from the burden of our individuality.

Accordingly, after discussing the implications freedom has for individuals in an individualized sociality, this chapter explores the idea of being together through the concept community. The reader will become aware that the key point about Bauman's story of 'being together' is its liquid modernity, and in terms of its community, it has to be understood as a state of mind, not merely because it is imagined in Anderson's sense,[10] but because sometimes we want to be in communities and other times we do not. The reader will see that myths are also central to these imagined, imaginary, unimaginable communities, since they provide the vessels within which the present moment and the past can be contained. Yet, as Bauman suggests, these intimations of community are painted only for individuals themselves. That they are painted for no one but individual selves is, too, part of their liquid modernity.

However, before any of this discussion can begin it is first of all necessary to consider Bauman's key argument that it is impossible to talk about concepts such as 'individualization' and 'community' without knowing something about the social conditions which gave rise to them. As the reader will see, for Bauman, if individualization is thoroughly modern, community is a set of social relationships associated with traditional society and we embrace it with such fever today – he argues that liquid modernity is the age 'of the lust for community, search for community, invention of community, imagining community'[11] – precisely because the truth is that there is no longer any such thing. In this regard, Bauman takes as his starting point Heidegger's idea that things only reveal themselves as important when they start to break, or when they go bust. And so it is with community, which for most of human history was thought of as 'always has been', as Raymond Williams once put it, but went bust when the incandescent modernity found that it had no need for a way of living conceived in a *zuhanden* world which was in the modern sense both backward and somnolent. Consequently, we shall see that what Bauman is suggesting is that the return to community in some alternative liquid form is not only challenged by the depredation of modern individualism, but that all dreams of community are bound to be racked with ambivalence because we inhabit a world in which individuals' aspirations for asserting their difference always take precedence over sameness. As the reader will see, in theorizing community in this way Bauman is, following Derrida, using the concept *sous rature*, only under erasure – 'in full consciousness of its departure from its conventional meaning'.[12]

THE *ZUHANDEN–VORHANDEN* TRANSFER

For Bauman, as for Marx, society is modernity and modernity is incessant change. Bauman also understands the crucial point that modern people do not have any sense of what Heidegger called *zuhanden Gelassenheit*, which is the capacity to simply let things be what they are, to leave them in order that they may sediment and acquire their own intractable existence – which eventually makes them into something like a community – as if they came into being of their own volition, or by divine ruling. The *zuhanden* kind of world is 'at once unchanging and arbitrary. Life must follow the ways of the past; and at the same time life cannot be planned … patterns of life are fixed in ways that cannot, must not, be broken just because they are traditional; at the same time unpredictable, unreliable, miraculous'.[13] In such a world the individuals were *embedded* in the local community, tied to the land where they lived and worked, and there would have been almost no possibility of them escaping their shared fate, because it was God's will that they stayed put.

As Bauman points out, it was humankind's discovery of culture which pulled it out of 'the dark expanse of *zuhanden* (that is "given to hand" and given to hand matter-of-factly, routinely, and therefore "unproblematically"), and transplanted it on to the brightly lit stage of *vorhanden* (that is, the realm of things that, in order to fit the hand, need to be watched, handled, tackled, kneaded, moulded, made different than they are).'[14] To use Foucault's terminology, the *episteme* which succeeded the preconceptual and presystematic *zuhanden* world was one underpinned by a solid modernist imaginary committed to unabashed system building. As we saw in Chapter Two, this modernity came with a world view after establishing first principles and foundations and a central organizing theme associated with social engineering. In the event the irrational *zuhanden* world was superseded by a rational and hegemony-seeking 'structured and structuring' world which like its predecessor eventually *seemed* to be set

> in its place before any human deed began, and lasted long enough, unshaken and unchanged, to see the deed through. It preceded all human accomplishment, but [in a way not even imaginable in the *zuhanden* world which preceded it] it also made the accomplishment possible: it transformed one's life struggle from an aimless tussle into a consistent accomplishment. One could add one achievement to another, follow the road step by step, each step leading, thanks to the road, to another; one could build one's accomplishment from the bottom up, from the foundations to the roof. That was the world of life-long pilgrimage, of vocation, or … of the 'life project'.[15]

Indeed, to be solid modern was to know a kind of security; it was to inhabit a world that *seemed* fixed and unchanging.

THE *VORHANDEN* TRANSFER MARK TWO

As Bauman continues to remind us, the time of solid modernity is no more and today the world we inhabit is increasingly governed by feelings of insecurity. As he points out:

> Twenty years ago eighty per cent of the working and earning people of Great Britain had secure jobs, insured against sudden and unwarranted dismissals and offering their holders a safe future in the form of welfare and pension entitlements; only thirty per cent can boast such jobs now, and the percentage goes on falling. Some countries try hard to stem the tide, but the prospects of success are not particularly convincing. In virtually every country the part of the work-force still enjoying the old security of employment is crumbling fast, while almost all new jobs are of the part-time, temporary, fixed-term, no-benefits-attached, and altogether 'flexible' character. Add to this the new fragility of family units, brittleness of companionship, fluidity of neighbourhoods, the breath-taking pace of change of recommended and coveted life-fashions and of the market value of skills and acquired habits – and it is easy to understand why the feeling of insecurity (better still: of *Unsicherheit* – that complex combination of uncertainty, insecurity, and lack of safety, best conveyed by the German term) is so widespread and overwhelming.[16]

In a nutshell, liquid moderns never stop struggling for security because they are destined to live their lives against a backdrop of relentless upheaval and change. Nothing – from jobs to relationships – in liquid modernity comes fully equipped or with a life-time guarantee. Consequently, if absolute security eludes liquid modern men and women, absolute anything else does, too. It's as if today they are forced to live their lives where the overall effect is analogous to shifting-sand dunes; just when you think you have got a foothold on a track, it slips away.

As Bauman suggests, if it was the onset of modernity which facilitated the transfer 'from the penumbra of *zuhanden* into the searchlight and spotlights of *vorhanden*',[17] it was the shift from solid to liquid modernity – the time of *vorhanden Gemütsbewegung* – which created a world that not only 'forbids standing still' but one which greets its incumbents daily and remorselessly with relentless change, what one might call 'a standing invitation, even a command, to act'. If Freud saw the modern world as a place where men and women were prepared to accept 'too little freedom in exchange for more security', Bauman switches the focus in the opposite direction. In a nutshell, he recognizes that with the *vorhanden* transfer Mark Two we have shifted from a structured and structuring society in which our identities were largely predetermined by the oppressions of solid modernity – in orthodox sociological terms, institutions such as social class, gender and 'race' – to a sociality in which individuality dominates more than anything else, and where identity always remains a work in progress: a sociality in which life is lived *noch nicht* surrounded by possibilities that have not yet been realized. In such a sociality self-transformation is not just a possibility – it is a duty. As Bauman puts it:

> In the last hundred years, the balance has shifted away from Freud's 'too little freedom in exchange for more security'. Now the pendulum moves, in full swing, in the opposite direction. Our common fears, anxieties and nightmares followed suit. Not the Orwellian vision of the jackboot trampling on human face torments us, but that of the trapeze act practised without a safety net ... Fear of inadequacy replaced the old horror of conformity. We fear more being left alone than being forced.[18]

Indeed, Bauman's story is one that runs opposite to the story that Freud kept on repeating – a story that was concerned with repression, or in other words, the idea that modern civilization was utterly reliant on individuals constraining their impulses and limiting their need for self-expression and knowing their place in the world. Bauman's story is one that is concerned with freedom and his idea is that liquid modernity is governed by a will to happiness, and to this extent it is a sociality in which the pursuit of individual happiness is held to be a legitimate right.

Bauman argues that whatever we do, our identities and lives are shaped for better or for worse by the pressures and ethos of liquid modern times and in anticipation of his critics he advises that his key point in making this argument is not to suggest that he thinks that the men and women of solid modernity

> lived daily with the knowledge of tightly structured time-space and the solidity and durability of the world – but that *we* live daily with the growing awareness that we cannot trust either. I am talking therefore above all about the present shock, not the past tranquillity. That past experience, as we tend to reconstruct it now, retrospectively, has come to be known to us mainly through its disappearance. What we think the past had – is what we know we do not have.[19]

FROM *HABITUS* TO *HABITAT*

What Bauman is suggesting is that being liquid modern means living and believing in ways other than those made tacit by one's own group's version of the already existing reality. In other words, *vorhanden Gemütsbewegung* is the essential quality of being liquid modern and this means that life is lived as if things have to be disquietingly and relentlessly 'made different from what they are'. Bauman's reliance on this existential version of human consciousness means that his sociology has little use for the concept of *habitus*, which in Bourdieu's schema is used to emphasize the central role played by the ineliminable significance of the individual's cultural framework in constituting his or her identity.

As is well known, Bourdieu suggests that the *habitus* is an embodied internalized schema which is both structured by and structuring of social actors' practices, attitudes, and dispositions.[20] The *habitus* also constitutes and is constituted by social actors' practical sense of knowing the world and it is through their 'feel for the game' that they come to see the social world and the position of themselves and others in that world as unexceptional. Vital to understanding this 'perfect coincidence' is the idea of the social actor's *doxa* values, which Bourdieu identifies with that tacitly cognitive and practical sense of knowing what can and cannot be reasonably achieved. In this sense, the *habitus* constitutes only an 'assumed world' captured as it is through the confines of the individual social actor's 'horizon of possibilities'.[21]

If Bourdieu's understanding of the idea of the *habitus* does not tacitly assume that the basic securities and affiliations of social class, custom, family and community that were established with the emergence of modern industrial capitalism for the most part still prevail, it does conjecture that there are objective structures which not only produce social actors but also their *doxa* relation with the world, or as Bauman puts it, the knowledge they think with, but not about. For Bourdieu, the *habitus* cannot be understood in isolation, and it along with different kinds of capital – for example, symbolic, cultural, social and economic – is indelibly linked with field. Fields reflect the various social, cultural, economic and political arenas of life, which form their own microcosms of power endowed with their own rules.

Without being inattentive to the point that some people 'are freer than others, some in being free in effect structure the world *for* others',[22] Bauman's sociology suggests that the concept of *habitus* is of limited efficacy, for understanding individual identity formation in liquid modernity because it fails to recognize that social actors today are hardly ever inhibited in their pursuit of their individual freedom. Consequently, he replaces *habitus* with the concept of *habitat*, which rather than being structurally determined, is

> a space of chaos and chronic *indeterminacy*, a territory subjected to rival and contradictory meaning-bestowing claims and hence perpetually *ambivalent*. All the states habitat may assume appear equally contingent (that is, they have no overwhelming reasons for being what they are, and they could be different if any of the participating agencies behaved differently) … The existential modality of the agents is therefore one of insufficient determination, inconclusiveness, motility and rootlessness. The identity of the agent is neither given nor authoritatively confirmed. It has to be construed, yet no design for the construction can be taken as prescribed or foolproof.[23]

Indeed, instead of being historically constituted in a given field of social life, *habitats* 'unbind' time and weaken the coercive impact of the past and 'the individual himself or herself becomes the reproduction unit for the social in the life-world'.[24] As Scott Lash suggests, this leads Bauman to suggest that the social actor is guided by 'a radical individualism … not a utilitarian but aesthetic individualism: not an individualism of a controlling ego but the individualism of a heterogeneous, contingent desire'[25] – which means that if liquid moderns are not all 'hedonistic sensation seekers', they are, each and every one of them, set with the task of making their own place in the world.

THE BUSINESS OF LIQUID MODERN LIFE

As we saw in Chapter Two, solid moderns had an inability to live their lives for the moment because they lived working towards the future perfect. Liquid moderns, in marked contrast, do nothing else but live life for the now. They are men and women who are in effect destined to live a life composed only of the present tense: 'a perpetual present with which the various moments of his or her past have little connection and for which there is no conceivable future on the horizon'.[26] As Wittgenstein pointed out, we do not want to know the future precisely in order that we can maintain our illusion of free will. Liquid modernity offers the sense not of some coherent and existentially understandable life but of the contingency of an unbridgeable gap between different realms of experience. In Bauman's liquid modernity there are few plans, and for the most part only hopeful contingencies. As a consequence, the 'business of life' separates into a series of choices, but this series:

> is not pre-structured, or is pre-structured only feebly and above all inconclusively. For this reason the choices through which the life of the agent is construed and sustained is best seen (as it tends to be seen by the agents themselves) as adding up to the process of *self-constitution*. To underline the graduated and ultimately inconclusive nature of the process, *self-constitution* is best viewed as *self-assembly*.[27]

In the event, *self-assembly* is no longer determined by tradition. Local customs that were once traditions become *relics* or *habits* and these only become collectivized as 'a result of generalizable influences of institutional reflexivity'.[28] In this sense, *habits* become manifest in configurations of consumer culture, but they are also more readily articulated in routinized forms of individual self-expression. In liquid modernity, men and women are forced to be above all else, at the same time, both rational and self-determined individuals (reflexive-selves). And the concepts of rationality and self-determination have two vital things in common; each puts the emphasis on the will of the *individual* rather than on the will of others. This combination of rationality and self-determination is what makes liquid modern men and women autonomous individuals – individuals *de jure* if not individuals *de facto* – judged responsible for their own individual choices and charged with the responsibility of the consequences of those choices. Being autonomous individuals also means that they 'are only partly, if at all, constrained in their pursuit of whatever they have institutionalized as their purpose'.[29] Bauman puts it even more unequivocally:

Let there be no mistake: now … individualization is a fate, not a choice; in the land of individual freedom of choice, the option to escape individualization and to refuse participation in the individualizing game is not on the agenda … As Beck aptly and poignantly puts it: 'how one lives becomes a biographical solution to systematic contradictions.' Risks and contradictions go on being socially produced; it is just the duty and the necessity to cope with them that is being individualized.[30]

With Bauman, sociology is made to recognize the individual; the human agent is returned to the centre of the picture and it is the world which they inhabit that 'makes (or does not, as the case maybe) the humans into *individuals*, rather than being a miraculous antidote to the terminal poison of immaculately conceived or "natural" and inborn individuality'.[31]

That life is individualized means that today people place a terrible burden on intimacy, from which there is no escape, and in his sociology Bauman captures a sense of the peripatetic, shifty and fragmentary existences of men and women who appear to live their lives as if they are perpetually on the run from themselves as they are from each other. In grasping a sense of this paroxysm, he recognizes that liquid modernity can be captured as much in people's relationships as it is in their possessions – and it is almost never satisfactory.

Bauman also suggests that the world we live in today is not the kind of place where you have to create your own drama, but you feel impelled to do so nonetheless. In this sense, he likens liquid modernity to a sociality where people are always on the verge of being struck by lightening: you never know where or when it is going to strike, only that it has happened. What he also insists is that getting struck by lightening is more common than people are prepared to imagine.

In this sense, liquid moderns are destined to live with ambivalence. They have needs that can never be satisfied because they do not always know what they need. So they try to live with their longings as best they can, which means feeding them with placebos of DIY transcendence. 'Rebranding' oneself and changing one's identity might feel like a revelation of sorts, but as Bauman might say, identities recast as 'brands' tend to be little more than consumer products, conveniently packaged and displayed for use by those wishing to acquire the latest lifestyle or by designers wishing to create one for them.

As we shall see, rather than some deeper reality, liquid modernity has the disturbing effect of feeling like some permanently unresolved and irresolvable moment in a parallel present, incapable of settling into anything more than a satisfying image that is always only going to linger 'until further notice'. Liquid modernity is in effect the gleeful dismantling of an orderly life: the perpetual disembedding and re-embedding. And accordingly, liquid modern lives are always going to be the fruit of contingency: of existential subjectivity and chance associations. Bauman is also suggesting that liquid modern lives are guided by a kind of existential self-consciousness, a reflexive idea of the self that can be understood as preternatural when it is thought of in relation to solid modern self-consciousness. In this sense, liquid modern self-consciousness holds its own ambivalence; it is both a threat and a promise. It threatens to upset the here and the now but it always promises new rewards.

LIQUID MODERNITY: A RHIZOME KIND OF LIFE

For Bauman, liquid modern living is rhizomatic; it is in a constant state of becoming: a middle without a beginning and an end. As he puts it, liquid modern living can be described as such because it 'seems to possess no sense of privileged direction, expanding instead sideways, upwards and backwards, with the same frequency and without detectable regularity which would enable a prediction of the next move. New stems arise in spots impossible to predict in advance'.[32] As I've suggested throughout this book, Bauman argues that in liquid modernity traditional forms of identity-making associated with social class and based on locality and community no longer prevail or have at least become what Ulrich Beck calls death-in-life zombie categories.[33] Liquid modern living is best seen through the metaphor of the rhizome because it is constructed as an open map – rather than the closed book of social class or any other kind of rooted or structuring way of life – and its features include incessant modifications to the identities and multiple social networks which tend to be associated with liquid modern lifestyles.

Rhizome lives also elude the dichotomies placed on them by structuralist sociologists because they are made by individuals whose decisions about which ways their lives should be lived are ambivalent through and through: for example, individuals who have a longing for roots but at the same time a need to escape them; immigrants who have to live with the sense of alienation and opportunity that comes from hybrid nationality; and even the comfortable majority who perceive that they are persistently under threat from insecurity, risk and danger, even though in material terms they have never been so comfortably off. Consequently, the liquid modern kind of identity has no deep structure and is 'so constructed that every path can be connected with every other one … [it] has no centre, no periphery, no exit, because it is potentially indefinite'.[34]

In liquid modernity, it is appearances that count and truth is performative. Identities might be formed in lives that are real enough, but they tend to be identities which are remarkably insubstantial and provisional or, to use one of Max Weber's metaphors, made of light cloaks rather than steel casings. Liquid modern identities are not solid because they are not quite identities. This is because liquid modern identity-making is concentrated on performing rather than building anything solid as such and in this way it thrives on its own ambivalence; it is always about performing an identity rather than expressing who you are.

For Bauman, as for Erving Goffman, the whole of society is on a stage and all of its members have to perform their identities. However, in a liquid modern sociality the idea that there is a division between a 'real' inner core and a somehow less authentic shell of an outer self *a propos* Goffman[35] no longer holds good. As Bauman puts it, drawing on Lyotard:

> We now live *open space-time*, in which there are no more *identities*, only *transformations* ... and the one thing lost is 'being' itself: it has no solid roots in time. Being, as it were 'is always escaping determination and arriving both too soon and too late' ... This is a time-space of the perpetual present and ubiquitous 'here'.[36]

Liquid modern identity thus has to be performed in the *dramatic mode*:

> a stiff scenario closely followed by the actors, but [this] stiffest of scenarios remains a scenario, a contrived text scripted in this rather than that way, and a text which could well have been scripted in that way rather than this; and even the most disciplined actors remain actors, playing their parts, this part rather than some other which they could play instead with the same flourish and dedication.[37]

Identities recast as transformations are remarkable performances which are rooted first and foremost in their isolation – an individualized sense of isolation at once unconscious, the fruit of a habitual DIY self-satisfaction dependent on the blessing of significant others, and finally the inevitable result of a newly achieved sense of self that grasps others without having to be grasped by them. The hope too is that their incumbents will find for themselves in these individualized identities somebody that is exactly itself and an image redolent of nobody else.

In this sense, liquid modern identities are best seen as productive and creative cartographies. The rhizome life is deemed the most appropriate way of living as it is 'entirely oriented towards experimentation in contact with the real ... it is detachable, reversible, susceptible to constant modifications'.[38] As Deleuze and Guattari might say, it is a life energized by a play of active and reactive forces, fashioned by the contours of a self-politics of desire, which makes self-transformation not merely a possibility but a duty to one's individuality. The liquid modern mentality is such that it perceives that life must be lived authentically and this is what makes life bearable and exhilarating. As Bauman suggests, liquid moderns follow Sartre's dictum: 'it is not enough to be a bourgeois ... one needs to live one's life as a bourgeois'.[39]

PALIMPSEST IDENTITIES

As Bauman points out, liquid modernity demands above all else a *palimpsest* identity 'which fits a world in which the art of forgetting is an asset'.[40] He suggests that, like the characters in the film *Eternal Sunshine of the Spotless Mind*, liquid moderns attempt to flush out all traces of memory in creating these palimpsest identities which are erased to make room for the next instalment. Indeed, according to Bauman, liquid moderns spend the best part of their lives rewriting themselves because perdurability is not the name of the game in liquid modernity. Consequently, selves become more than the sum of their parts; the individuals you see do not really determine who they are and what they do together. Contrary to postmodernism's depthless asocial individuals who have no identities to speak of – either because they have disappeared into discursive formations or have become merely representations – Bauman's individuals are always being themselves. For Bauman, what remains uncertain is not our identity but our knowledge of it and the problem is that, because they live in an era of constant change and disposability, individuals not only seem to have too many selves to choose from, but they have developed an extreme dislike for performing the same identity too often.

One life strategy employed by liquid moderns for reconciling this turbulent existence is to live parallel lives which have little to do with one another. Identity in this sense is about disassociation, a mysterious division between the real and the hyperreal. In liquid modernity it turns out that there is not one but many aspects to the self, projected through a lens which unites them to create the image of one identity. But this is an identity without a centre, a meeting point. And the more you watch you wonder how some of these different aspects of the self could be so different, how sealed and impenetrable to each other they might appear.

Liquid moderns believe single-mindedly that any pain or alienation they may have to face in the name of this constant reinvention of the self is not only worth it, but that it ensures the solitude they imagine they need in order to live their lives to their full potential. Liquid modern identity making is an art form and they are artists. Moreover, each one of them is deadly serious about and deeply committed to their creative work. They are people capable of devotion, but true to form that devotion is, like Narcissus's reflection in the pool, aimed straight at themselves. Self-obsessed with how they look, liquid moderns turn to self-help manuals for wisdom and sound advice about how to live their lives. This is a matter not just of self-protection but of aesthetics; liquid moderns believe that their individual difference is paramount, and to perform their individuality is a mark of their authenticity.

Liquid moderns are constantly on the look out for the immediacy of the sting of pure transcendence, outside all previous experience. The trick is to conceive an identity so swift and slight that it seems as weightless as the fantasy that made it. In this sense they are like the characters of Milan Kundera's fiction, who have to live with the burden of being confronted with inexorable change and with fantastical powers of weightlessness, winging their way through life, their quest is to attain a temporary but bearable lightness of being. This results in a liquid version of the ritual performance of perpetual rebirth. Quick-fix transformation, the sort that results from a new job, a different lover, meeting up with the 'girls' or a night out with the 'lads' is ubiquitous in liquid modernity. There are simply so many competing loyalties with identity that it becomes, for the individual, a site of weighty ambivalence as identity's superbly elastic work finds itself pressed into yet another role.

In a liquid modern world satiated with difference, new selves soon become, for the market, uneconomical, and for individuals themselves, boring. The accoutrements of recently acquired identities – the holiday-maker, the exciting lover, the trendy image – once the catalyst for a splendid metamorphosis, soon become instead prison wardens whose mere presence is a constant reminder of our captivity. For this reason, liquid moderns are continually compelled to begin the process once again, stealing away into new selves, where once again they can experience the possibility of becoming all things. And so this process goes on. For Bauman, this process of contingent self-creation is racked with a sense of ambivalence of existence and he challenges us to confront the reasons for this ambivalence. This is because Bauman understands what the ambivalence associated with struggle for self and identity in liquid modernity is really about. He realizes that it is the struggle, not the end itself, what liquid moderns 'really, really' want, what they 'totally' get off on. They are all searching for that elusive feeling of the transcendental. By making new identities they believe they can remodel their histories as well as their current lives, but whenever they do they quickly find that the new identity, within a short space of time, is no better than the one they have been trying to fix. We can therefore conclude that in

> our world of rampant 'individualization', identities are mixed blessings. They vacillate between a dream and a nightmare, and there is no telling when one will turn into the other. At most times the two liquid modern modalities of identity cohabit, even when located at different levels of consciousness. In a liquid modern setting of life, identities are perhaps the most common, most acute, most deeply felt and troublesome incarnations of *ambivalence*. This is, I would argue, why they are firmly placed at the very heart of liquid modern individuals' attention and perched at the top of their life agendas.[41]

LIQUID MODERN RELATING

Bauman also points out that if one's foremost commitment is to the idea of a palimpsest version of the self, to the idea that self-transformation is only just over the horizon, commitments of a more enduring, interpersonal nature are simply not going to happen. And if liquid modern men and women's identities are going to be contingent and temporary, so are their relationships. In liquid modernity, relationships are only made to be broken. Liquid moderns seem to have an inbuilt ability to short-circuit the need for others. But this is not surprising in a bloated consumer sociality where everyone has opted for ease and convenience. As Bauman puts it:

> Bonds are easily entered but even easier to abandon. Much is done (and more yet is wished to be done) to prevent them from developing any holding power; long-term commitments with no option of termination on demand are decidedly out of fashion and not what a 'rational chooser' would choose … Relationships, like love in Anthony Giddens's portrayal, are 'confluent' – they last (or at least are expected to last) as long as both sides find them satisfactory. According to Judith Baker, author of bestselling 'relationship' handbooks, most relationships are designed to last no more than five years – enough time to pass from infatuation through the attachment phase and land down in the 'why am I here?' phase. With partnerships and other bonds in flux, the *Lebenswelt* is fluid. Or, to put it in a different idiom – the world, once the stolid, rule-following umpire, has become one of the players in a game that changes the rules as it goes – in an apparently whimsical and hard-to-predict fashion.[42]

Bauman captures in his sociology the peripatetic, fragmented and uncertain lifestyles of men and women who it would seem are as much on the run from themselves as they are from each other. Bauman suggests that this state of affairs is related to the all-pervasive nature of consumer culture in liquid modernity; when you get habituated to a consumer world where immediate gratification is the norm, your capacity to make long-term commitments is undermined. And it seems as if liquid moderns are terrified that committing themselves to another will plunge their lives into deep freeze, in the process depriving them of new experiences, all their individuality lost.

Liquid moderns soon get bored of lives that are always meant to be permanent, but all too often end up being provisional. Indeed, if liquid modernity removes individuals from the anchors that initially form them, it also encourages separation, valorizes solitude and aloneness. In his sociology, Bauman persistently explores how human frailty and loneliness affect men and women today. Liquid moderns live with an intense ambivalence; on the one hand they want to be natives and feel part of the community, while on the other they deny themselves the possibility of being truly integrated because of their own self-perceived otherness – in other words, their individuality. Correspondingly, what we used to call relationships are 'progressively elbowed out and replaced by the activity of "relating"'.[43] Liquid moderns are the unacknowledged masters of ambivalence; they give passionate lip service to their desire for pure relationships while secretly avoiding them at all costs. Bauman is suggesting that this has something to do with liquid modern culture's enduring love affair with personal transformation, coupled with the mistaken notion that committing to a loving relationship has the power to stop the very thing that led to that relationship dead in its tracks. By relying on social relations that are no more than short-lived encounters, they can also maintain a sense of distance from themselves, safe in the fantasy that the life that they are living is itself only a temporary dissatisfaction, one from which, if they hold their breath long enough, they will emerge intact.

Living in liquid modernity also means living with the knowledge that not only the Other but also that you yourself is not necessarily the person you thought you were. Liquid moderns yearn for the kind of control that self-mastery brings, but the reality is that they change their minds an awful lot. This is first and foremost because liquid modernity is a relentlessly changing world that pivots around unexpected contingencies, which are more often than not 'felt' as epiphanic, and which tend to open into other worlds. As Bauman suggests, these quotidian moments often catch their victims unaware, their impact and consequences time and again rendering individuals about to fail themselves and others for whom they are responsible. Swept along by an unseen current, they find themselves in deeper and deeper water, amid the debris of old routines and half-remembered snatches of great times once lived, the wreckage of past lives the only things worth hanging on to (in a world that is forever on the move, even the most recent aspects of the past seem as if they happened a long time ago).

As Milan Kundera might say, in liquid modernity life seems as if it is elsewhere, life seems much more interesting where other people are at. The grass always seems greener on the 'other' side. In liquid modernity everything seems to be a teasing reminder of something else worth pursuing. This is why liquid moderns are always apt to fall in and out of relations, friendship, marriages. Life simply seems to throw them into those situations and you never know what is going to be around the corner: some crush, some attraction or some new infatuation. Bauman's idea of a free sociality is one in which the social, cultural, economic and political conditions of democracy enable everybody to lead lives of their own choosing but he is very much aware that the ambivalence of liquid modern living means that one person's freedom – today more than ever before – often means another's suffering. By the law of unintended consequences one person's freedom can end up wreaking another's sense of personal turmoil.

There is always a sense of an impending contingency in liquid modern ways of relating – the feeling that you could be living a different love story from the one your partner is experiencing. As a consequence, liquid moderns have to live with the threat of existential insecurity. This is often caused by the decisions of individuals to act or not act in situations in which they find themselves. For example, think of the married academic who never ever had any intention of leaving her partner of 10 years, but did after she was blown away by a drunken kiss she had with a professor of feminist theory at a sociology conference during the summer recess. Sure, these kinds of situations affect people differently, but Bauman's sociology brings to our attention the point that people can and do act on the spur of the moment, without any thoroughgoing reasons, and that if these actions tend to lose their sense of arbitrariness in the wider scheme of things, they could always be different. The academic still loves her partner, but she also feels she must leave him for the woman she has just fallen in love with. What this means is that Bauman recognizes that our own individual freedom to choose often manifests itself as both a blessing and a crime.

He recognizes, too, that when these relating episodes end they never actually do finish – even for the departing partner's want of trying. There are always the residues which go on past their endings: heartbroken ex-partners and children as well as the personal hurt and guilt – innumerable remains: untidy, messy, and wasted. It is hoped that these freeze-framed revelations will simply melt away, from one identity to the next – sometimes with a wink to something more lasting, more likely not. This kind of life may be punctured by bouts of incredible hurt, but – and here's the rub – the pain is worth it because of the passion and the intense ephemeral happiness it brings, which is heightened by the hovering threat of another ending, another rejection. Drama, like other forms of excess, however emotionally exhausting, tends to be highly addictive.

Many of these speeded-up separations, just like the new encounters they are replaced by, are nothing more than about liquid modern men and women finding themselves and to this extent they come across as individuals who have not quite grown up and who are in a hurry trying to make up for it. It is speed that is the point – the urgent transubstantiation – the way that one identity or relationship disappears just as it begins to take a seemingly solid shape. Speed is the driving force. This is why the idea of the 'virtual' is the perfect metaphor for liquid modernity because it is a world without boundaries in which all the traditional markers of linear narrative – time, place and fixed identities – are being constantly dissolved. Liquid modern identities may on the surface appear to combine an immaculate surface veneer with sinews of hardened ice, but these are always ready to liquefy at the slightest whiff of some new appeal. Liquid modern relationships, like liquid modern identities, are all too often magnesium-flare-like: all of a sudden lit and quickly over. As Bauman puts it:

> The advent of virtual proximity renders human connections simultaneously more frequent and more shallow, more intense and more brief. Connections tend to be too shallow and brief to condense into bonds. Focused on the business in hand, they are protected against spilling over and engaging the partners beyond the time and the topic of the message dialled and read – unlike what human relationships, notoriously diffuse and veracious, are known to perpetrate. Contacts require less time and effort to be entered and less time and effort to be broken. *Distance is no obstacle to getting in touch – but getting in touch is no obstacle to staying apart.* Spasms of virtual proximity can be, both substantively and meta-phorically, finished with nothing more than the press of a button.[44]

Indeed, liquid modernity is a text message sociality in which a random text message can generate all manner of emotional, existential, epistemological or transcendental chaos. That liquid modern men and women are the arbiters of their own fates is something that Bauman constantly reminds us of, and that the paths of their lives are freely chosen is something each and every one of them realizes and this realization is what makes their chosen life modes ambivalent at every turn.

Bauman is suggesting that the experience of living in liquid modernity is not so much like riding a rollercoaster or juggernaut, in Giddens's meaning,[45] as trying to tread water in a torrent of waves of which you are forced to ride the troughs and swells, each rush of surf presenting another predicament, another quandary. Swept along by an unseen current they are unable to anticipate, liquid modern men and women often find themselves in deeper and deeper water, amid the debris of old routines and half-remembered snatches of lives which only yesterday seemed new or 'happening', but today feel merely like a series of dim stories in the head, almost fictions, disturbing performances of the imagination, the remains of past lives the only things left and the only things worth hanging on to.

Liquid modernity is a world that unsystematically erases all freshly laid traces of 'social structure' before they have even had time to sediment into anything more substantive, and it is from these erasures that its energy is derived. As we have seen, Bauman shows us that living in liquid modernity is 'permeated with a sense of ambivalence of existence, the contingency of events and the insecurity of being'[46] and as Chris Rojek has argued, the fact that liquid modern individuals are reflexively aware of the utter meaningless of their own sense of place in the world means that all too often self-dissatisfaction and ennui become overwhelming features of their existence.[47] Liquid moderns are in effect that ambivalent eccentricity: superficially self-confident but fundamentally insecure individuals. In terms of dealing with the latter, it is to community that they invariably turn because it is perceived as as good a peg as any on which to hang their individualized hopes and fears. As the reader will see, one of the strengths of Bauman's analysis in this regard lies in its ability to demonstrate the pivotal role that community plays as something of an unreliable remedy for overcoming the insecurities and anxieties lurking beneath the surface veneer of liquid modern identities.

LIQUID MODERN COMMUNITY

'Words have meanings: some words, however, also have a feel', Bauman tells the reader at the beginning of *Community*. 'The word "community" is one of them. It feels good: whatever the word "community" may mean, it is good "to have a community", "to be in a community"'.[48] Bauman is not saying that the word community and the meaning of community as it is experienced in the already existing reality are the same thing of course. He is too astute a sociologist to do that, not only because unlike many other commentators he is able to hold at bay the twin threats of sentimentality and nostalgia that tend to blinker most analyses of community,[49] but also because he knows that the idea of community provokes for sociology many questions.[50] But he is sure of one thing: the liquid modern version of community consolidated into reality is nothing but a second best, 'poor man's' replacement for the 'real thing'; a concept which is 'known for being perpetually defiant of reality that would not bend to its shape'.[51]

Drawing on Hegel's famous dictum that 'the owl Minerva begins its flight only with the onset of dusk',[52] Bauman suggests that we embrace community with such fever precisely because in reality there is no longer any such thing. There is no such thing as community in liquid modernity because there exists no solid ground under which the conditions of a community could ever be realized. We can 'imagine' community with sociology's grey in grey only because we think it 'always has been'. What Bauman means in this regard is that if sociologists are really interested in saying something useful about 'community', they should be honest enough to speak about 'community' as it is lived, as it is experienced, today. They should be writing about the 'transformation of "community"' or the 'appropriation of "community"' instead of fumbling around in the ashes of something that in effect is broken, caput, gone. As he puts it:

> Community can only be numb – or dead. Once it starts to praise its unique valour, wax lyrical about its pristine beauty and stick on nearby fences wordy manifestos calling its members to appreciate its wonders and telling all the others to admire them or shut up – one can be sure that the community is no more … 'Spoken of' community (more exactly: a community speaking of itself) is a contradiction in terms.[53]

As we have seen, Bauman argues that liquid modernity is experienced as speedy, fleeting and transitory and liquid modern men and women are in effect *disembedded* from what sociologists might have once upon a time called the local community. With liquid modernity, a postulated unity of interests gives way to more specialized *habitats* and associated lifestyles and individuality, and men and women become '*operators* who are willing to forego a secure source of fruit for a chance to connect more of the world'.[54] Individuals going their own way in a world tend to hook up with other individuals with whom they share common interests to form what Bauman, after Maffesoli,[55] calls neo-tribes. In this sense, liquid modern communities are nothing more than self-defined communities, conceptually formed 'by a multitude of individual acts of *self-identification*'.[56] Sucked as it has been into the soft melt of liquid modern identity-making, community itself is but an individualized expression: individually constructed for individual needs.

Neo-tribalism is not so much about community as about looking for a new identity, a sense of identity that is not available to individuals elsewhere, and it is significant to them not so much because they are on the look out for anything deep or substantial to belong to, but because they have become bored or more likely threatened by the demands on their individuality. Liquid modern men and women are in truth the unacknowledged masters of ambivalence – giving passionate lip service to their desire for 'togetherness' while secretly avoiding it at all cost – their experiences reflecting the contradictions inherent to the liquid modern condition in general.

Bauman suggests that this fascination with community should not really come as any surprise to us because of the outstanding legacy of the Reagan/Thatcher years which saw a societal turn towards greater privatism, individualism and social polarization. In this sense, liquid modernity perhaps inevitably had to become an age of community, because the world had turned itself into one of increasing *Unsicherheit*. Into the bargain *Unsicherheit* had become the responsibility of the individual, or in other words all doubts and fears had become private property. In which case, for Bauman it was bound to happen that with liquid modernity would come a need for community. The imagined, imaginary and unimaginable community appeals precisely because it takes liquid moderns away from the burdens and anxieties of the now into an imaginative space where everything is sure and nothing is in crisis. Their attempts to bring 'home' the warm feel of a community and unfolding it before themselves is as much as anything else an attempt to hold back liquid modern change, to stop the world from running away and taking them with it.

However, as Bauman points out, the liquid modern yearning for togetherness manifests itself in forms which vary considerably from the model of community promulgated by orthodox sociology. In liquid modernity, community is merely *imagined* to offer an assemblage of 'self-assembly kits' as a means to make our 'DIY escape'[57] from the manifest *Unsicherheit*. For Bauman, then, liquid modernity does not a signal the re-emergence of the Tönnies type *Gemeinschaft* community, rather it replaces rootedness with strolling, playing, tourism and vagabondage. Liquid modernity is a *vorhanden Gemütsbewegung* world in which community has gone bust and its 'gaping void is hastily filled by [what he calls] "peg communities", "ad hoc communities", "explosive communities" and other disposable substitutes meant for an instant and one-off consumption ... They quench the thirst for security, albeit briefly. None is likely to deliver on the hopes invested, since they leave the roots of insecurity unscathed.'[58]

Community is like an enormous peg on which these dreams of belonging are hung, like a succession of wreaths. As each wreath withers it is replaced by another. What all liquid modern forms of community have in common is a sense of depthlessness and impermanence; 'like in the case of many other commodities purchased for sale, the durability of the goods is less than fully guaranteed and the customer's rights are less than fully honoured'.[59] Bauman's understanding of liquid modern community is that it is really only a metaphor about the relationship between the individual and the world outside themselves. It is nothing more than a nourishing antidote to a thoroughly individualized life. Thus his argument has an underlying discourse which suggests that imagined community relationships are ephemeral surface phenomena, destined to disappear as people move between social groupings and have 'no other firm ground but the members' commitment to stand on, so communities live as long as the attention of the members is alive and emotional commitment is strong. Otherwise they simply vanish.'[60]

If community is still there in liquid modernity, it is there in the sour taste of its own absence. Yet this is not community lost in the way imagined in the orthodox sociological literature. There can be no absolute loss in a world without absolutes and which is marked by its sense of perpetual recurrence. Community is something unimaginable which, like everything else in liquid modernity, is simply recycled. This understanding of community is different to orthodox sociological accounts in another way too; and Bauman argues that it is not so much adversity but consumer culture that is the glue that binds liquid modern people together, apart.

Yet this doesn't stop liquid moderns living with a permanent feeling of homesickness and longing for a feeling of home. Consequently, liquid modern life is pregnant with the wish to settle into some kind of together-ness – to slip under togetherness's safety blanket of certainty and engagement – which community holds out as its promise. Part of the reason why that wish is so urgent is because of the larger problem with whole enterprise, which is that liquid moderns know deep down that the settling they are wishing for never occurs.

Homesickness is in this sense is hyperreal; liquid moderns do not really long for a home that has been lost; they instead long for something outside themselves that they do not have, or haven't yet been able to find. Homesickness is also a kind of nostalgia that is hardly ever about the past and more to do with felt absences or a sense of something lacking in the present. In liquid modernity the past doesn't really matter because consumer culture has the ability to take people back to a time and a place even if they were never there in the first place. What is more, the ways of relating that are inbuilt in liquid modern communities are ones that we do not always expect and are ones which can take us by surprise; sensational and breathtaking in their intensity, they often feel like relationships with people you have known for a long time even before you have met them.

Liquid modern belonging is essentially about men and women sharing with others the products of their collective imaginations – imagination is what liquid moderns have in bucket-loads – which allows an aggregate of alone individuals to share some kind of image of belonging. As a symbolic marker of something unattainably marvellous, community is a cumulative product of the imagination of like-minded but essentially different individuals at different times, continually reclothed and reinterpreted, and always representing the same challenging human aspiration. All that really matters to a liquid modern contemplating community is its surface sheen and it is as if there is a faked intensity given to what was once seen as ordinary lived human relations. Even at their onset these are social relationships which are already beginning the slow petrification into myth.

THE APPROPRIATION OF COMMUNITY

Community as social exclusion and social control

In that indispensable lexicon of the 'language of cultural transformation', *Keywords*,[61] Raymond Williams suggests that what is perhaps the most important feature about the concept of community is that it never seems to be used unfavourably; and that people show a tendency to use it in a 'warmly persuasive' sense to describe existing or postulated forms of social organization. The notion of community as an integrated, local social system comes from traditional society; and in many respects, it is this impression of the term that symbolizes what, for many, community represents: the antithesis of modernity; if modernity is about anomie, then community is about belonging and togetherness. However, what Bauman also suggests is that if community implies a temporary safe-haven from our anxieties, it also implies social closure and exclusion for those who are not 'one of us'. As he argues, although the 'community narrative' seduces its adherents with ideas of warmth, belonging and togetherness, the reality is all too often the reverse:

Community advertises itself as the cosy, burglar-proof home amidst the hostile and dangerous city; it draws profusely, overtly or obliquely, on the very contemporary image of the sharp divide between the fortified and electronically protected homestead and the street full of knife-carrying strangers ... the self-proclaimed wardens of its purity ... divide good from evil, and for better or worse dictate the definition of moral conduct. The paramount concern of their moral legislation is to keep the division between 'us' and 'them' watertight; not so much the promotion of moral standards, as the installation of double standards ... one for 'us', another reserved for the treatment of 'them'.[62]

For Bauman, the empirical truth of community is that for social groups to exist collectively they need to differentiate themselves from other social groups in order to achieve their sense of collective identity. As Fredric Jameson puts it: 'the nascent collectivity seems necessary to have to define itself by way of frontiers and borders, by way of a kind of secession: it must always, in other words ... posit an enemy'.[63] In bringing our attention to this most pernicious aspect of community life, Bauman is clarifying what divisions can be like when communities commit themselves to adhere to a set of values in such an emphatic sense. And as he indicates further, the result of such tyranny and absolutism is *oppression*, which results from the 'pressure to keep the intended flock in the fold ... the craved-for cosiness of belonging is offered as a price of unfreedom'.[64]

Bauman goes further to suggest that oppression is carried out through strategies that do not merely seek to exclude outsiders, but also to polarize them. Borrowing from Lévi-Strauss, Bauman argues that at every level of society, social groups employ, conjointly, *anthropophagic* and *anthropoemic* strategies of oppression towards outsiders; the two strategies are only effective precisely because they are used in conjunction. Communities employing *anthropophagic* strategies gobble up, devour, and assimilate outsiders who they perceive to carry 'powerful, mysterious forces'.[65]

In marked contrast, those employing *anthropoemic* (from Greek: to vomit) strategies towards outsiders, metaphorically throw them up, casting them into exile, 'away from where the orderly life is conducted ... either in exile or in guarded enclaves where they can be safely incarcerated without hope of escaping'.[66] The two strategies work as one:

The phagic strategy is *inclusivist*, the emic strategy is *exclusivist*. The first 'assimilates' the strangers to the neighbours, the second merges them with the aliens. Together, they polarize the strangers and attempt to clear up the most vexing and disturbing middle-

ground between the poles of neighbourhood and alienness –
between 'home' and 'abroad', 'us' and 'them'. To the strangers
whose life conditions and choices they define, they posit a genuine
'either–or': conform or be damned, be like us or do not overstay
your visit, play the game by our rules or be prepared to be kicked
out from the game altogether. Only as such an 'either–or', the two
strategies offer a serious chance of controlling the social space.
Both are therefore included in the tool-bag of every social
domination.[67]

Community as consumerism

What community also stands for in liquid modernity is a freeze-framed
representation, merely the click of a lens on a fluid, fleeting landscape of
temporary togetherness, whose pattern is always shifting from one event
to the next – who or what is currently in favour with the public: the death
of a princess, a cup final, a charity concert, the list is unlimited. In this
sense liquid modern community has a gift for yoking personal enlightenment to entertainment. Though not really tied to tradition, liquid moderns
recognize a need for habit – if not ritual – through which individuals can
come to know themselves and honour those like them. Sports fans, for
example, have such ceremonies through which they excel at creating their
own sense of symbolic community.

In this sense, community is 80,000 people in the open air on a May
afternoon at the Millennium Stadium in Cardiff lustily singing along to
'You'll Never Walk Alone', united with the rest of their 'community'
through television and the incessant text messages, communicating who's
scored. The liquid modern version of the sport fan community is not the
'terrace' crowd of yore, but is one inhabited by individuals who are
repulsed by the thought of the 'disease and toxic substances' that they
might come into contact with if their bodies touch or get too close to
other men and women they don't know and don't really want to get to
know.[68] This is a community that comes to life in the all-seater stadium,
which with the architect's forward planning is co-extensive with the liquid
modern imagination in its capacity to bring individuals together – 80,000
individual spaces that accommodate 80,000 individuals for only 90
minutes – who with the help of a compere, some razzmatazz and a big
screen running the highlights of the spectacle in hand, are ushered through
a series of emotions that are all to do with the performance of community.
The liquid modern football ground is a site where fans can individually
perform their allegiance to their team like extras on a film set. In this
sense, they are an ersatz but demonstrably performative community of

individuals seeking individual attention while getting some time off from the uncertain and risk-sodden world of liquid modernity. This spectacular version of community may seem something like an enclosed world, but this is not the kind of community which remains binding and compelling long after it has disintegrated.

In its sport and leisure manifestations, liquid modern community is a copy so closely modelled on the real thing that it even has the ability to send shivers down the spines of anyone who is taken in by its appeal. It seems authentic, something like the equivalent, which hints at deep themes, but which turns out to have only a depth of hidden shallows: a superb imitation, but one entirely free of the demands of the 'real thing'. This kind of community may be inauthentic, but Bauman acknowledges that in its magic moments it can turn the quotidian into something ethereal, particularly when it takes place in alcohol- or ecstasy-fuelled circles, for example, in pubs and clubs.

This is also the kind of community that is ambivalent through and through; its members can be irresponsibly individualistic, they can drink and take drugs, be 'loved up', and at the same time feel deliciously at home, both together but apart. As I found in my own study of the leisure life-world of 'the lads' in Leeds, its members can have a community of sorts which although it comes *without any harsh demands on their commitment* allows them to

> have a 'solid' modern leisure life coupled with a 'liquid' existence. A 'solid' life, which has gone but is redeemable and a 'liquid' existence, now, which has to be endured. There the leisure life-world operates, tucked snug, if a little out of place, into the weekend nightlife of Leeds. It could simply have grown of its own accord, you feel – made from the very heart of Leeds. As if it were very much a production of a time and a place, suspended in the nightscape like a time capsule, with its machinery intact, in spite of everything around it humming their own different tunes.
>
> The ultimate appeal of this leisure life-world for 'the lads' is that for each of them it fulfils both a need, which is their mutual longing for 'home' and 'security', and a concomitant desire for the quotidian of the non-rational – in the form of leisure, play and pleasure. For 'the lads', the leisure life-world is *the* pivotal point in a fragmented life, which allows them to fashion a sense of order out of the disorder of the everyday world of liquid modernity. The price of the freedom offered to 'the lads' by liquid modernity is the loss of a fixed cultural identity, which must subsequently 'be

searched for and somehow restored'. And it is through the leisure life-world that they set about this restoration process.[69]

If liquid modern community is something that is appropriated by ordinary men and women in liquid modernity, it is also something that is readily appropriated by transnational corporations such as *Starbuck's*, *McDonald's*, *Coffee Bean* and *Burger King* and there it can be found 'abroad' in what Marc Augé calls those non-places,[70] where you can feel at home away from home. In his book which charts the meteoric rise of the global coffee chain *Starbuck's*, John Simmons tells the tale of how its marketing executive, Howard Shultz, found a 'warm' place in the hearts of its young and upwardly mobile customers by simply recognizing their collective need for something like the coffee house 'experience' seen on the U.S. TV programme *Friends*.[71] What Simmons essentially argues is that *Starbuck's* was quick to recognize that its major customers are the lonely *Friends* generation who have a collective need for something to belong to and what it has been very clever at is creating for them in its cafés a sense of *chez nous* found at the *Friends'* favourite coffee house *Central Perk*.

What Simmons fails to consider in his analysis is that the marketing executives of global companies like *Starbuck's*, who by the nature of their occupations have been robbed of their own local culture, have themselves a need to put a global head on community and at the same time they have the ability to shake off this head, as if knowing instinctively when to feel global and when not. This last point notwithstanding, what Simmons's analysis does astutely demonstrate is that at *Starbuck's* ordinary men and women can become, fleetingly, *Friends* characters: Chandler, Joey, Monica, Phoebe, Rachel and Ross at *Central Perk* – an aesthetics of social interaction which is a pseudo-community, a shadow community, a community of merely like-thinking consumers.

As Bauman points out, these versions of community as consumerable substitutes have the edge over the 'real stuff', because like other consumerables they promise

freedom from the chores of endless negotiation and uneasy compromise; they swear to put paid to the vexing need for self-sacrifice, concessions, meeting half-way that all intimate and loving bonds will sooner or later require. They come with an offer of recuperating your losses if you find all such strains too heavy to bear. Their sellers also vouch for an easy and frequent replacement of goods the moment you no longer find a use for them, or when other new, improved and still more seductive goods appear in sight.

In short, consumerables embody the ultimate non-finality and revocability of choices and the ultimate disposability of the objects chosen. Even more importantly, they seem to put us in control.[72]

Indeed, what all of these versions of community appropriated thrive on is the contingency of community without responsibility; they couldn't operate without it.

In the light of the above discussion we can perhaps conclude that if liquid modern communities are not communities in the orthodox sociological meaning, they are at least their poor relations – perhaps old aunts or distant cousins. And what this means is that Bauman can agree with Benedict Anderson[73] that liquid modern community *can be* conceived as a deep-felt mutuality, albeit temporarily. He also agrees with Anderson that community is imagined in the sense that it is limited by its strictly demarcated, though elastic, boundaries; beyond which lie ways of being and living that take the form of various threats, anxieties and uncertainties. Bauman also knows that like Anderson's imagined community, liquid modern community is sovereign, because it came to maturity at a parti-cular stage in history when freedom was hardly unequivocal. However, he also knows that its stage in history is not the same as Anderson's – when freedom was only a rare and much cherished ideal – it is a time when freedom depends on one's ability to consume. Indeed, as we shall see in the next chapter, in this regard Bauman suggests that if today freedom means happiness, liquid modern men and women are never happier than when they are consuming.

5

Consumerism as the Liquid Modern Way of Life

If our ancestors were shaped and trained by their societies as producers first and foremost, we are increasingly shaped and trained as consumers first, and all the rest after.

Zygmunt Bauman[1]

In the *Sage Dictionary of Cultural Studies*, Chris Barker's first definition of consumption simply suggests that to consume is 'to use or ingest'.[2] Without actually saying so, Barker goes on to add that the process of consuming is better understood as consumerism because this second concept recognizes the economic and cultural dimensions that underpin the different uses to which the commodities that circulate in capitalist societies are put. In this regard and in keeping with most other interpretations of consumerism in cultural studies,[3] he suggests that consumers do not merely consume commodities like unsuspecting dupes (or dopes), but they 'generate their own meanings through the interplay of commodities and [their own] cultural competencies'.

It must be noted that what is missing from Barker's definition is any recognition of the culture of excess associated with consumerism which in its oversupply leaves innumerable endings, untied and messy – wasted lives as well as wasted commodities. It is conspicuous too that in Barker's definition consumerism is not understood as an all-encompassing reality – it appears instead as a powerful belief system but one that can be transgressed or resisted because there are other alternative belief systems that vie for people's attention in latter-day capitalist societies. In this sense, Barker plays down Bauman's argument that today we are all 'consumers in a consumers' society. Consumer society is a market society; we are all in and on the market, simultaneously customers and commodities'.[4]

However, the intention of Bauman's theory of consumerism is neither to ignore the point that some people endeavour to transgress or resist the pervasive consumer culture nor to accept *vis-à-vis* Baudrillard that the production society of solid modernity has been superseded by a depthless and hyperized asociality where individual agency is irrelevant and where the illogic of a consumer 'code' reigns supreme over subjective ideas, marking the victory of the 'anti-social sign over the social sign'.[5] On the contrary, and as we have seen throughout this book, for Bauman, the 'real world' and the people who inhabit it are always drumming insistently on each other's doors.

In this chapter, I want to suggest that the strength of Bauman's analysis is not so much in the way he sees consumer culture as an all-encompassing reality, but the way in which he suggests to us that if we are prepared to admit that consumerism has become *the* way of life we are in a better position to learn a great deal about the 'means and the mechanisms' of the liquid modern sociality, which means of course that we will also be better equipped to do something about changing the world for the better, for humanity.

In response to this challenge, I consider here two important themes relating to consumerism in Bauman's work: that of social control and that of the relationship between consumerism and intellectual work. In relation to the former I explore the changing nature of social control with the shift from a producer society to a consumer sociality, while with regard to the latter I critically discuss the implications of consumerism for sociology and the conditions this places on the development of intellectual activity. In the first instance, however, it is necessary to briefly consider in more detail the meaning of consumerism. As the reader will see, if in Bauman's eyes liquid modernity is far from being a hermetically sealed universe, he sees it as an all-consuming playpen of consumerism which is so pervasive that it not only 'becomes the social link between the life-world of individuals and the purposeful rationality of the system as a whole',[6] but also takes on the character of a eusociality or a 'swarm', whose personnel mechanically stick to their mission to consume without the need of 'commanding officers, marching orders and daily briefings'.[7]

CONSUMERISM IN A CONSUMER SOCIALITY

As Bauman puts it, consumerism 'stands for production, distribution, desiring, obtaining and using, of symbolic goods.'[8] It is an over-the-counter culture that is as loud and shiny as lip gloss and which evokes a world in which image is piled upon image with the relentless impersonality of a comic strip come to life. Consumerism is also what various commentators have described as Disneyfication, Nikeization and McDonaldization all at once. It exists in the real of the city as well as in the irreal of cyberspace; it is on advertising hoardings, in shop signs and on the internet. It exists in the pace of everyday life: in popular culture, in the instantaneity of fast food, in the waist-lines of bloated consumers, in fast cars, in the muzak piped through the speakers in the myriad shopping malls. It exists on the emblems of t-shirts, jeans and trainers just as it exists in the language of the streets where it can be heard in the voices in the crowds: 'you want us to consume – OK, let's consume always more, and anything whatsoever; for any useless and absurd purpose'.[9]

In the event, people's emotional engagement with consumer culture is all-pervasive in liquid modernity. Liquid moderns are men and women who possess and are possessed by consumer culture and like the characters in Georges Perec's classic novel *Les Choses* (*Things*) they live their lives through the objects they buy and consume. They find it desperately difficult to leave the crude, fervent world of consumption behind and as a consequence they are destined to live their lives on the surface; they have to, since there is nothing much below it. They have no credible history that they are aware of – only the nostalgia for a marketwise DIY ready-made historicity – and no culture other than a consumer culture that is their own.

As has been remarked by numerous social historians, by the middle of the eighteenth century Britain had created its own 'empire of consumer colonies'. What Bauman's sociology suggests is that at the turn of the twenty-first century, Britain, in common with most other countries in the west, has become an 'empire of colony consumers' – everything from Japanese and Korean TVs, DVDs and computers and Taiwanese and Indonesian-made sports wear, to Indian cuisine, Italian chic and American culture. According to Bauman, consuming has today become an obligation rather than simply a choice; the globalized world we inhabit is a realm of great shoppers who take great pleasure in acquiring commodities.

However, the possession of commodities is, as Bauman suggests, 'only one of the stakes in the competition'.[10] What we also need to grasp is that there is (no)thing that is uncommodifiable in liquid modernity. As Bauman points out in his most recent work,[11] the consumer industry has even at last found 'the bottomless and self-replenishing gold-mine it has long sought' in the commodity of fear, which he goes on to argue is for the consumer industry a 'fully and truly renewable resource', to the extent that it 'has become the *perpetuum mobile* of the consumer market – and so of the present-day economy'. Nowhere is this commodification of fear better illustrated that in the mock documentary film, *Fahrenheit 9/11*, where Michael Moore gleans ironic amusement from the security devices now sold to American consumers panicked by the 'war on terror': the steel 'safe rooms' which protect purchasers in the safety of their own homes and the specially designed harnesses for abseiling to safety down a burning skyscraper.

Bauman also alerts us to the point that consumer culture involves a kind of symbolic rivalry over the meaning of commodities and 'the differences and distinctions they signify'.[12] In this process, commodities themselves necessarily acquire an unlasting aura – an ephemerality wrongly described by some critics as planned obsolescence – which the market endlessly recycles to make anything from feel-good films to innocent songs that take their watchers and listeners back to some past golden era. In this way consumer culture not only allows the past to be 'up-graded' in the light of new experiences but it cannily permits nostalgia without necessarily depending on it.

If the major accomplishment of the centred 'roots of order' underpinning solid modernity was to turn life into a regimentality in which the work of *homo faber* and the leisure of *homo ludens* was divided,[13] the major accomplishment of the decentred disorder-sustaining liquid modernity has been its ability to turn the attention of *homo faber* and *homo ludens* to the life of *homo consumens*.[14] Indeed, as Bauman argues, it is the instantaneity of consumer culture and its ability to 'take the waiting out of wanting' in delivering *homo consumens*' hopes and dreams that is today what is imagined as the measure of the success of a life worth living.

Of course consumption has always been with us. But the consumption that the majority of people of the time of solid modernity knew was a different but equally discriminatory kind of consumption. It was a disease, otherwise known as tuberculosis, which ate the body from within and was what the poorest 'producers' of solid modernity used to die of. Consumption in liquid modernity is, on the other hand, a disease of spending from without and is one the 'flawed consumers' of today would gladly like to suffer, would happily die for. If solid modernity was for the majority of people a world with the problem of living with reduced circumstances, liquid modernity is one with the problem of living with excess – a world of endless choices. An apt aphorism for liquid moderns is that they expect to do everything to the full. They certainly know how to do excess: drink, food, sex, shopping – whatever and wherever.

As I pointed out in the last chapter, the individual liberated through reflexivity is burdened with choice, and is at every turn faced with the need to make decisions; it is up to the individual to choose the life they think is best. In their droves, liquid modern individuals, according to Bauman, are now free to choose, choose to consume. In a consumer culture the market plays on people's desires and wishes to be entertained and as such, life becomes a cycle of developing and fulfilling desires and wishes.

Bauman is suggesting that consuming is *the* way of life. We can shop both at home and away – we even have TV channels dedicated to home shopping when we cannot be bothered going to the shopping mall – but going to the mall has a special kind of pleasure all of its own. As Walter Benjamin might have said, the 'event' of the shopping experience, at the moment of its realization, is everything, since it incorporates pleasure, such pleasure that pleasure is not a word capable of identifying with the kind of pleasure that shopping brings. Don DeLillo's novel *White Noise*, at once mocking and applauding about consumer culture, captures well Bauman's sense of ambivalence towards the freedom offered by consumption, and the following description, which elucidates all of the juicy significance of shopping for consumers in a consumer culture, deserves to be quoted at length.

The book's main protagonist, Jack Gladney, is galvanized into shopping mode by one of his fellow teaching staff at the 'College-on-the-Hill', Eric Massingdale, who he meets for the first time outside work in the Mid-Village Mall. Eric, who is intrigued by Jack's off-campus choice of clothing, tells him, 'with a grin turning lascivious, rich with secret meaning', that he has the look of a 'big, harmless, aging, indistinct sort of guy'. The encounter awakens Jack to the significance of his own invisibility – which, as Bauman might say, is the damning dread of all liquid modern men and women – and it puts him 'in the mood to shop':

> I found the others and we walked across two parking lots to the main structure in the mid-village Mall, a ten-story building arranged around a center court of waterfalls, promenades and gardens ... into the elevator, into the shops set along the tiers, through the emporiums and department stores, puzzled but excited by my desire to buy. When I could not decide between two shirts, they encouraged me to buy both. When I said I was hungry, they fed me pretzels, beer, and souvlaki. The two girls scouted ahead, spotting things they thought I might want or need, running back to get me, to clutch

my arms, plead with me to follow. They were my guides to endless well-being … We smelled chocolate, popcorn, cologne; we smelled rugs and furs, hanging salamis and deathly vinyl. My family gloried in the event. I was one of them, shopping, at last shopped with reckless abandon … I shopped for its own sake, looking and touching, inspecting merchandise I had no intention of buying, then buying it … I began to grow in value and self-regard. I filled myself out, found new aspects of myself, located a person I'd forgotten existed … I traded money for goods. The more money I spent, the less important it seemed. I was bigger than these sums. These sums poured off my skin like so much rain. These sums in fact came back to me in the form of existential credit. I felt expansive, inclined to be sweepingly generous … I gestured in what I felt was an expansive manner … Brightness settled around me … we ate another meal.[15]

As Bauman sees it, for liquid moderns as for Jack Gladney, consuming is what makes life palpable; this is because individually it makes liquid moderns feel visible, and it has the ability to show them what happiness looks like. In this sense he recognizes that consumer goods are not simply objects; consumers see themselves in them. In the manner of Lyotard,[16] Bauman observes that consumption is no longer of objects, but of *consumptions*. As we saw in the last chapter, the slipping away of the certitudes that once seemed to go with solid modern lives is what leaves liquid modern men and women vulnerable and hankering for promises of paradise. But if consumption is about the individuals' long-term love affair with themselves, it is first and foremost through the acquisition of consumer goods that individuals perceive that they can best transform themselves. As Linda Grant puts it:

Because how you feel when you have your new coat or wrap dress is something so mysterious, complex and potentially transformative that it is almost metaphysical. For a new coat can induce not only happiness but a radically revised sense of who you are. You can call this by some piece of jargon if you wish, you can invoke phrases such as 'self-esteem', but they don't encompass the whole vast empire of the self. The new coat makes things possible. It casts you in a new light to yourself.[17]

In this regard, it is important to recognize Peter Beilharz's point that Bauman's sociology prompts us to recognize that 'even in consumption there is creativity of action, for culture is praxis'. But as the same author calls to our attention, 'Bauman's purpose here is to alert us to the contrary, that to consume in the dominant social forms of today is also necessarily to conform. It is always the dark side that threatens us.'[18] Bauman recognizes that consumer culture begins where authenticity leaves off, ends, ceases to exist. It inhabits a different territory, which is a marketized, featureless, cultural desert and individuals recast as consumers for the most part live in that desert.

But the wonderful thing about consumer culture is just that: it is consumptive, nothing more than an excruciatingly staged performance act. It is for the moment. As Bauman points out, with consumer culture things 'must be ready for consumption on the spot; tasks must bring results before attention drifts to other endeavours; issues must bear the fruits before the cultivating zeal runs out. Immortality? Eternity? Fine – where is the theme park where I can experience them, on the spot?'[19] And you can do anything with commodities – if you can afford the cost. Consumer culture is compelling in a profound way because it works ingeniously through strategies of entertainment, with comprehensive engagement not required. Indeed, as clearly demonstrated in the quotation from *White Noise*, what is celebrated in liquid modernity is the unextraordinary moment, that familiar individualized quality of consumption, which Bauman argues is the defining existential feature of liquid modernity.

SOCIAL CONTROL IN A SOCIALITY OF CONSUMERS

Bauman draws on the theory of surveillance associated with Foucault to suggest that, in liquid modernity, consumer culture has emerged, for the masses, as the new 'inclusionary reality' or precarizing constraint. Like Foucault's other critics, Bauman also conveys in his work an unmistakable critique of this model of surveillance.[20] Unlike these writers, however, he theorizes the relationship between power-knowledge and social control anew, resolving to understand social control in the present rather than in the past. I will discuss these two aspects of Bauman's theory of liquid modern social control presently, but it is first of all necessary to outline the rudiments of Foucault's model.

As is well known, in his seminal theorization of modern social control, *Discipline and Punish*, Foucault used a startling juxtaposition to provide a graphic representation of the unfolding of the machinery of survcillance in what he described as a new disciplinary society.[21] In so doing he suggested that in solid modern societies there has been a historical movement from brutal and overt repression to rational, scientific and bureaucratic social control of 'deviant' populations through surveillance. In this most illuminating work, Foucault evoked the image of Jeremy

Bentham's Panopticon in order to argue that the all-seeing 'gaze' (*le regard*) comes to serve as a metaphor for surveillance connected with governmentality in the modern state.

A significant feature of the Panopticon is that like George Orwell's[22] *Big Brother* surveillance, it is indiscernible; those under surveillance are always unsure whether or not they are being watched. This model of surveillance keeps those being watched subordinate by means of uncertainty and as a consequence the 'watched' simply act in accordance with the Panopticon, because they never know 'when' or 'who' might be watching. Foucault argued that these social controls – the panopticonisms of everyday life found in schools, hospitals, factories as well as in the more obvious places such as prisons and military barracks – micro-manage individuals more efficiently than the carceral systems of yore because they thwart deviant behaviour through self-actuating prohibitions reinforced by the subject's own certainty in the omnipresence of the all-seeing power of the gaze.

Although the work of Foucault initially held much promise in overcoming the growing disenchantment with the problems of the more established understandings of social control, there were soon exposed a number of theoretical and empirical difficulties in adopting an alternative perspective for exploring social control which was at once anti-foundationalist, anti-scientific and anti-humanistic. Consequently, in recent years social control has become controversial; it floats indecisively between applications and critiques of the Panopticon model; it suffers from severe problems of legitimacy because the power of the state and other large social institutions has diminished in significance, at the same time the ability of individuals to say no has spectacularly increased.[23] Indeed, however beguiling Panopticon social control was in its attempts to make the oppressed complicit in their own repression, in liberal democracies it inevitably invited reaction and something had to give. Subsequently there has emerged a reticence to engage with the concept at a theoretical level and it has become little more than an aphorism for a theory, which gives sociologists a way out when all else fails.[24]

As I have argued elsewhere, sociologists of deviance and criminologists alike have in the main moved their focus away from ideology, theory and abstract thought and as a consequence more recent analyses of social control have been concerned with the ways in which public perceptions of crime have become sensitized to danger and how the right to censure as a result of 'dangerization' has come to feature more extensively in crime control.[25] For example, Lianos with Douglas considers this new way of thinking as a 'tendency to perceive and analyse the world through categories of menace', which invokes the tacit assumption that the world 'out there' is unsafe.[26] The upshot is that social control has become managerial rather than curative.

The demise of Big Brother Mark One

In developing his own critique of Foucault's Panopticon model, Bauman argues that the configuration of economic arrangements associated with consumer capitalism has become of crucial importance for explaining patterns of social control today. To put it another way, social control like much else in liberal democracies has by and large been commodified and privatized. As Bauman points out, Panopticon social control assumes an 'ordered and reason-led society' reflected in the nation states which emerged and grew in solid modernity.[27] As he puts it:

> One can hardly imagine a group more strictly differentiated, segregated and hierarchic than the population of the Panopticon ... Yet *all* residents of the Panopticon – the Overseer, the supervisors and the lowliest of the inmates alike – are *happy*. They are happy because they live in a carefully controlled environment, and thus know exactly what to do. Not for them the sorrows of frustration and the pain of failure.[28]

However, as I argued in Chapter 2, Bauman shows us that the comfortable majority no longer live in the shadow of tyranny of the state; instead they create their own paroxysm, driven by market forces that they have no authority over, but at the same time have no final authority over them. Liquid moderns live in a sociality where taste and aesthetics are all-pervasive and everything is always up for grabs. Bauman argues that the kind of life offered by consumer culture appeals most of all because it is perceived to be a life of freedom and the unwillingness to take on the trappings of being grown-up; at the same time, however, it is a challenge to the social hierarchies which prevailed in solid modernity.

Inequality in a consumer sociality, inequality in a casino culture

As we have seen already, liquid modernity operates with a system of power and a hierarchy which on the surface of things is no longer conferred by the orthodox sociological stratifications of social class, gender and 'race'. The freedom liquid modernity celebrates is the personal freedom to consume: the freedom to live and to love without social interference, to cross social class, gender, culture and ethnicity divides in the search for personal fulfilment. In this sense, the collective unconscious of the masses is no longer tied to social stratifications associated with the solid modern producer society but expertly tuned into the essential purpose of private consumption, like the toy-town demeanour of the vast out-of-town shopping malls it so much resembles.

Bauman argues that in liquid modernity private consumption replaces work as the backbone of the reward system in a sociality which is underpatterned rather than patterned, disorganized rather than ordered. It is only the poor – the 'flawed consumers' – who are still controlled through the work ethic. Bauman argues that liquid modernity is a predicament that breeds new forms of inequality and servility. It is consumer culture that is today the central unequalizing tenet, which takes shape in the market place, telling individuals when, like Coca-Cola, they are the 'real thing'. It is a hypermarket of hype. Just as the market is ruthless in the way it does business, so the transnational corporations are rootless in their national, communal and moral allegiances, and unabashed in their contempt for culture. Because of globalization, international trade, slacker border controls, cheaper and quicker forms of travel, and the internet, all the countries in the world today share resources and affect each other. And the losers in this process, the 'flawed consumers', not only lack the competencies for work, but the capacity to be accomplished shoppers.

To put it simply, liquid modernity redraws the boundaries between social class divisions as a relationship between those who happily consume and those who cannot, despite their want of trying. What Bauman is suggesting is that it is exclusion rather than exploitation that is the watchword of repression in liquid modernity. Social control is barely noticeable, except for the flawed consumers, whose subordinate position prevents them from participating freely in what has become for the masses a dream world of consumer culture. Instead of being repressively control-led, this fragmented society is driven by Freud's 'pleasure principle'. To be a consumer is to escape the problems of blood and social class; in a consumer culture hierarchy only exists in the power of advanced capitalism to create images of the system people spend all their time trying to aspire to or stand apart from. Liquid men and women realize too that they are no different from anybody else and that to perform their individuality is the only game in town. Consequently they are destined to live a life as a 'casino culture', that 'wants from you nothing but to stay in the game and have enough tokens left on the table to go on playing.'[29] A life that is messy, uncertain, fragmentized, ongoing, a skein of dangling opportunities and chances – a dice-life which is as fathomless as the sea and where everything seems as if it happens by chance – and this has the paradoxical effect of making life appear in a way that nothing happens by chance, that everything is fated.

To reiterate, the solid modern pecking order lies in ruins because, in a casino culture, life is a game and no one social class, gender or ethnicity can make use of every opportunity on offer. To a large extent, to be a consumer is to escape the problems of social class, 'race' and ethnicity or gender; in a consumer culture hierarchy exists in the power of advanced capitalism to create images of the system people spend all their time trying to aspire to or stand apart from. The principle features of this liquid modern kind of social stratification are, for Bauman, obvious enough: no *apparent* inequalities as such, no *apparent* solid modern narratives, no *apparent* social class, racial or patriarchal hierarchies. Yet the consequences of this type of sociality allow for new, more insidious forms of social control, which are not endowed with any of the coherent or identifiable structures of domination outlined in more orthodox sociological accounts.

The duplicity of consumer culture

Nonetheless Bauman is aware that in liquid modernity individual identity-seeking is a form of dream-making that is pathetically absurd. The idea of individuality, like authenticity, emerges at its most potent when it transpires that there is no such thing; existentially individuals may be unique, but uniqueness or 'being' the 'real thing', is fated to be no more than fleetingly significant in the marketized consumer culture that is liquid modernity. In the event, individuals set themselves a circle that they can never hope to square; the ambivalence of being authentic in a consumer culture where authenticity is just another lifestyle choice. Yet this does not and nor could it prevent individuals seeking out the significance of their own personal individuality through the task of performativity, which is brought on by the damning fear of invisibility. What is more, it barely matters that the DIY lives made in liquid modernity, with their rhino skin aesthetics, look and sound like a lot of other lives; it is something about the mood that those lives instil that makes them feel so utterly fresh.

Shadowing the very freedoms that liquid modernity names as consumerist are the consumer inequalities which the market tries to disguise. For Bauman, if liquid modernity is constructed through consumption, we are all consumers today, and it takes a 'heroic constitution' to concede that one is not part of the consumer game.[30] The upshot of this is that liquid modern inequalities are cast as consumer inequalities; in a sociality of consumerism you are what you can afford. Consumers appear to be free to choose any life-style they wish, because the market flaunts consumer choice so lavishly. However, the purported equality perpetuated by the free market forcefully dupes the masses by hiding the accomplished inequalities of consumers, even though these inequalities are materially visible to even the untrained eye.

The old adage that private freedom thrives on public squalor is as relevant today as it has always been, but as Bauman[31] suggests consumer capitalism gives an undertaking to deliver what it cannot – equality. The market disciplines some – notably the flawed consumers – and like the national lottery provides a week-in-week graduated roll-over prize to be shared unequally amongst the others. Differently from its predecessor, production-orientated industrial capitalism, consumer capitalism is bereft of any openness and honesty – at least with industrial capitalism you pretty much knew where you stood.

Bauman accords consumer capitalism a second two-facedness. It reduces the notion of freedom to consumerism; it leads people into thinking that they can liberate themselves by simply choosing a new identity. Consumer capitalism

> puts the highest premium on choice: choosing, that purely formal modality, is a value in its own right, perhaps the sole value of consumerist culture which does not call for, nor allow, justification. Choice is the consumer society's meta-value, the value with which to evaluate and rank all other values. And no wonder, since the 'choosiness' of the consumer is but a reflection of competitiveness, the life-blood of the market. To survive, and even more to thrive, the consumer market must first shape the consumer in its own image: the choice is what competition offers, and discrimination is what makes the offer attractive.[32]

Although consuming seems to be something to celebrate, Bauman suggests that the freedom it brings comes with a sad undertow. In this sense, the echo of an older, familiar grievance rings through Bauman's theory of liquid modernity; the rational humanism of the Enlightenment led to a shallow, self-centred materialism which today manifests itself most noticeably in consumer culture. A long time before Bauman was charting contemporary consumer culture, Adorno and Horkheimer,[33] two of the most perceptive philosophers of modern times, were suggesting that it is not possible to separate human consciousness from the material existence of people's lived condition. And they offered their own theory of the modern world, which if it suggested that the chaos we live in today originated in America where a religion of serial consumption was established along with the idea that continuing acquisition of ever better-looking, better-performing material goods makes life perfect, also suggested that everything we see is mediated through the filter of the 'culture industry'.

As is well known, Adorno and Horkheimer asserted that we may think that we are free, but we are only free 'to choose an ideology – since ideology always reflects economic coercion – everywhere proves to be freedom to choose what is always the same'. But as I have said already, if for Adorno and Horkheimer it was 'monopoly' and 'sameness' that were the two important defining features of the 'culture industry', in liquid modernity it is the search for 'polysemy' and 'difference' which defines individuals' roles as consumers and their 'rebellion' is more personal and consumptive than ideological and productive.

What Bauman does stress, *vis-à-vis* Adorno and Horkheimer, however, is that having liberated modern men and women through consumer culture, liquid modern capitalism keeps them performing the same forced choreography *ad infinitum.* An endless fresco of more of the same, and a sameness from which the mind and eye keep a distanced refuge and a world in which nothing very distinct is expressed but then again where lavishly borrowed and recycled images are always designed to shock, to excite, to keep the consumer curious – liquid modern aesthetic, that once became established, simply took over. A fantasy league of men and women jumping free of the burden of their solid modern history, which, *contra* Marxism, could not have been anybody else's intention. The other problem with this is the lack of competition for consumers' attention. There is only so much consumers can do with commodities; there are only so many ways you can achieve incongruity before you get bored with trying. For Bauman, these consumer identities appear to be torn from time, from the here and now, and brought together in an all-together-now chorus. For all its surface glamour, consumer culture is as shallow and empty as the shelves are seemingly bottomless and full to bursting in the stores which comprise the out-of-town shopping malls.

Even the men and women who were incapable of knowing consumer culture in their youth are seduced by its instant availability in liquid modernity. And like other consumers they have no intention of changing the world, they just want to enjoy being in it. In the unlikely event that they were ever to make a vow, it would be to never grow up. As Emma Soames, the editor of *Saga Magazine*, recently pointed out, no social group is

> more obsessed by youth than the new old [those who came of age in the 1960s], who display a gritty determination to cling to the culture they invented. Scared of nothing but death and dependence, they are using the toolkits of trusted brands, cosmetic surgery and the culture of youth to stay young. They are prepared to go the distance on the running machine to stay in the playground of youth. They are turning up the volume and getting on the dance floor.[34]

If older liquid moderns do not mature well, their younger counterparts do not do childhood well either. Their behaviour is always that of someone a different age to themselves; adults behave like teenagers and teenagers behave like adults. Wrapped up with consumer culture is the subversion of linear narratives, such as age and time so that we can be 40, a teenager, parent and grandparent all at once. All of this is not so much motivated by resistance to anything as such but simply by a wish to break free from the fixities which accompany more predictable forms of identity and the life course; and it is in the untidy realm of consumer culture that these always-in-progress cultural dynamics tend to metamorphose.

Superseding ethics with aesthetics and the evasion of the public realm

Bauman also recognizes that Adorno and Horkheimer were right when they suggested that the masses live in an infantilized world for much of the time – cushioned by prosperity, only occasionally awakened into difficult ethical choices of maturity – which is not to say that there is never time for direct political drama. As Bauman points out, in a consumer world, liquid moderns live perpetually on the edge of change and there is always demand for drama. Even here, though, direct action is usually no more than play-acting, however well intentioned. Voices are insistent on being heard, but as Bauman observes, these tend to belong to the television, not the political platform or the polis.[35] This is because in liquid modernity 'it is aesthetics, not ethics that is deployed to integrate the society of consumers, keep it on course, and time and again salvage it from crises. If ethics accord supreme value to duty well done, aesthetics put a premium on sublime experience'.[36]

In liquid modernity, aesthetics are worth more than knowledge and wisdom and because they draw on a heritage soaked in surface rather than depth (aesthetics rather than ethics) liquid moderns become the real-life incarnations of Baudrillard's cult of the 'into', who are obsessed with 'forms of appearance and become dedicated to the utopia of preservation of a youth that is already lost'.[37] They also expect the celebrity faces on their television screens – which on the one hand peddle the wares of the consumer capitalism and on the other feel the need to confess to us their every depravity and addiction – to be youthful and wrinkle-free. The celebrities are perceived to be the miracle of the liquid modern obsession with self-construction, not least because they are the 'stars' who give hope to ordinary people who long to reinvent themselves. In this sense it is clear to see why liquid modernity is also the age *par excellence* of makeovers and botox because its incumbents 'naturally' believe that lines on the face are unpleasant on the eye – as well as being a constant reminder of mortality – and it makes perfect sense to airbrush them out of sight. This aesthetic impulse also makes perfect sense because liquid modernity is a world where theatricality and the childlike delight in pretending go hand in hand – as Lyotard might have put it, the idea of performativity is coterminous with the new 'generalized spirit' of knowledge in liquid modernity.

If consuming is the stuff of dreams in liquid modernity it co-exists with a hopeless evasion of the public realm. Bauman brings to our attention the point that at the present moment in time liquid moderns are likely to be neither independent-minded individuals nor interdependent-citizens but slavering dogs more accustomed to shopping and too busy-minded towards consuming to be bothered by the messy particulars of politics. To paraphrase Pyotr Chaadaev: the minds of liquid moderns reach back no further than yesterday; they are, as it were, strangers to themselves ... That is a consequence of living in a consumer culture that consists entirely of imports and imitation. They absorb all their ideas ready-made, and therefore the indelible trace left in the mind by a progressive movement of ideas, which gives it strength, does not shape their intellects ... They are like children who have not been taught to think for themselves; when they become adults, they have nothing of their own – all their knowledge is on the surface of their being, their soul is not within them.[38]

The great French novelist André Gide may have found wisdom in Antoine de Saint-Exupéry's[39] demonstration of the 'paradoxical truth' that 'man's happiness lies not in freedom but in his acceptance of duty (sic)'.[40] But as Bauman reminds us, when that duty is toward shopping – as it is in the liquid modern sociality – much more than the happy shoppers' contentment to shop is at stake. It is the threat of losing the hard-won citizenship rights, which until their emergence in modernity were restricted to only the most privileged social groups, that are most at risk. As Bauman puts it:

> The truth is that the consumer's skills, indeed, rise at the same time as the citizen's ineptitude and, ultimately, the citizen's impotence. The 'consumer's skill' consists in seeking biographical solutions to socially-produced afflictions; to use a metaphor – it consists in fighting a nuclear threat by purchasing a family nuclear shelter, or pollution of drinking-water supplies by finding a reliable brand of bottled water. Consumer skills emphatically do not include the art of translating private troubles into public issues, and public interests into individual rights and duties – the art that

constitutes the citizen and holds together the polity as the congregation of citizens.[41]

When 'things don't go as planned', citizens recast as consumers are naturally inclined to blame the manufacturers rather than taking responsibility of putting things right themselves. As Bauman points out, it as if 'we have been trained to stop worrying about things which stay stubbornly beyond our power ... and to concentrate our attention and energy instead on the tasks within our (individual) reach, competence and capacity for consumption.'[42] Liquid moderns are free, but existentially they are stubbornly bound by their dedication to consumer culture. For the majority, freedom consists of little more than deciding whether to eat at McDonald's or Burger King, shop at Sainsbury's or Asda, buy their furniture at Ikea or Habitat, or fill their car up at Shell or BP. Consumer culture, with its bland, uniform ubiquity, has a sameness and wherever you go there will be Britney Spears playing in the background and the world's local bank, HSBC, will do nicely thank you. But even this lack of surprise and suspense does not seem to dull their propensity to shop.

If in Adorno's administered society[43] consumer culture felt like a violation of what life was meant to be, in Bauman's liquid modernity it seems more and more like life itself, as life should be. Consumerism seems to have everything going for it, because more than anything else it makes consumers feel free. But if men and women recast as consumers act as if they are overtaken by a sublime confidence, it is one that has a surprising absence of responsibility. Consumers might operate with a feeling that they are flying on automatic pilot and as obstacles present themselves, so adjustments have to be made, but these are made with the caveat that as consumers they do not really have to get involved. Like Lyotard, Bauman insists that there is something performative and wished about liquid modern living. It is a privatized kind of theatre, in which the larger sociality provides the parts, but doesn't directly cast the play. But rather than being a public world proper, this sociality of individuals is a performance of individuals who perform their lives and continue to do so even when their individual circumstances dictate otherwise. But the real problem is that it is a consumer culture that robs individuals of the responsibility of the stewardship, which if they were prepared to look for it, would make them the architects of their own destinies.

Seduction and repression

Bauman argues that, contrary to the postulations of the critical theory of Habermas,[44] in the liquid modern sociality, the 'weapon of legitimation'

– the hegemony by which the state acquires its *raison d'être* – has been supplanted 'with two mutually complementary weapons: this of *seduction* and that of *repression*'.[45] For Bauman, as for Giddens,[46] 'experts' and 'expert systems' play a crucial role in liquid modern sociality, but not in Habermas's sense. They are no longer needed to serve the needs of capitalism to 'legitimate' the dominant hegemony; rather, they become crucial to the enforcement and preservation of the weapons of *seduction* and *repression*.

For Bauman, as for Foucault, it is the poor who continue to experience the hard edge of exclusionary and repressive surveillance. As Bauman points out, '*repression* [still] stands for "Panoptical" power, as described by Foucault. It employs surveillance ... and is indispensable to reach the areas *seduction* cannot, and is not meant to, reach'.[47] A crucial role that *repression* carries out in this respect is to elucidate the unappealing traits of non-participation in the realm of the free market, by reforging 'the unattractiveness of non-consumer existence into the unattractiveness of alternatives to market dependency'.[48]

Ultimately, it is the prevailing presence of *repression* that manifests itself in the form of the welfare services – the reforms that once aimed to destroy the 'five giants' of want, disease, squalor, ignorance and idleness – which makes *seduction* the secure vanquisher in this game of domination. Rather than being emancipatory, the welfare services today constitute a second-rate and repressive regime, which have recourse to the expert and governmentalized 'gaze' of those employed by the state: the DSS officer, the community development worker, the GP, the social worker, the probation officer, and so forth who collectively 'police' the 'flawed consumers'. In Feeley and Simon's terms this approach is 'concerned with techniques to identify, classify, and manage groupings sorted by dangerousness. The task is managerial not transformative'.[49] What we see with this trend is plain and simply the criminalization of poverty. To illustrate his argument, Bauman points out that in

> New York for instance, in the five years to 1999 the police budget rose by 40 per cent, and the police force by 12,000 officers, while the social service budget went down by 30 per cent and the number of social workers by 8000. In California, the penitentiary budget rose between 1975 and 1999 from $200 millions to $4.3 billions, while the sums dedicated to social assistance fell by 41 per cent.[50]

As Bauman suggests, this repressive kind of social control, which always operated with a sense of detachment, is today made possible through the death-in-life zombie institutions of the state which just about have the necessary authority to command the power-knowledge of governmentality. For Bauman, cool distance is of the utmost importance here since social control is not merely used to differentiate 'us' from 'them', it also allows 'us' to construct 'them' as 'the objective of aesthetic, not moral evaluation; as a matter of taste, not responsibility'.[51] This process is what Bauman describes as idiaphorization, which if it signals 'the removal of certain classified groups from the spheres of moral concern and competence',[52] it also essentially marks the comfortable but anxious majority's disengagement with a commitment and responsibility for those who do not conduct themselves as 'we' do.

Watching the celebrities or the making of Big Brother Mark Two

Be that as it may, Bauman argues that since in liquid modernity the market has accomplished its ideal of 'making consumers' dependent on itself',[53] the *repressive* apparatus of the Panopticon has largely been supplemented by the *seductive* allure of Synopticon watching. Drawing on the work of Thomas Mathiesen,[54] Bauman argues that in the liquid modern sociality it is by and large not the few *who watch the many* (Panopticon), but rather *the many who watch the few* (Synopticon) and the few who are most keenly watched are the celebrities, who

> may come from the world of politics, of sport, of science or show business, or just be celebrated information specialists. Wherever they come from, though, all displayed celebrities put on display the world of celebrities – a world whose main distinctive feature is precisely the quality of being watched – by many, and in all corners of the globe: of being global in their capacity of being watched.[55]

In Bauman's liquid modernity, Debord's *Society of the Spectacle*[56] does not so much give way to Baudrillard's *Third Order of the Simulacrum* – that is the 'hyperreal' does not supersede the distorted 'real' – rather the *Society of the Spectacle* is succeeded by one of celebrity, what Nicholas Bourriaud has called the 'society of extras, where everyone finds the illusion of an interactive democracy in more or less truncated channels of communication.'[57] As we have seen, the flawed consumers are the neglected underside of liquid modernity, the silent emblem of poverty, which brings together the sub-themes of social exclusion, obesity and human waste. The overside is represented by the celebrities, that deafening coterie of consumer culture, which brings together the opposite sub-themes of inclusion, skinniness and consumptive waste, who exist to remind us that we could be all these things if we, too, were so fabulously successful. But celebrity has its own ambivalence; it is ordinary and special, within reach but somehow, at the same time, out of reach, of some other world. However, this does not stop ordinary men and women themselves wanting to be famous. A recent survey in the UK found that 'being famous' is the number one ambition of most children under 10 years old and that 'we have moved into a celebrity culture so strong ... being famous is an end in itself'.[58]

Celebrities in their pre-modern form were understood as icons and as such relics of divinity, but consumer culture merely bleeds them for sanctity. In the age of liquid modernity, celebrity 'spectacles' – anything from divorces, to deaths of princesses, to football matches, to larger-than-life episodes of soap opera stars' 'real' lives – take on a special role. They offer 'that something missing' by proxy: a surrogate memory, a surrogate significance, a surrogate solemnity, a surrogate community – a surrogate 'anything you want'. In this way, celebrities succeed in creating an audience in their own image, a tribe hardened to the modes and manners of heightened fandom. As Schickel has suggested, that celebrity has the power to create these kinds of myth is what makes it all the more enticing. The idea of celebrity is of particular significance because, as he suggests, celebrities are often represented by the media as a small and cohesive group of individuals, who in their fame or notoriety share close communal ties, no matter how different their routes to stardom.[59]

Social control: from normalization to precarization

What is also significant about the Synopticon, however, is that unlike the repressive apparatus of the Panopticon it 'needs no coercion' – it is the substitution of celebrity for everything else that has fed this phenomenon. With the Synopticon come 'new' and 'cool' ways of imagining life as it ought to be lived which supersede the discourses of power-knowledge associated with the 'work ethic' and 'scientific truth', which undergirded the Panopticon as Foucault imagined it. If the ambition of Panopticon surveillance was situated in its repressive exercise of power-knowledge, the success of decentred Synopticon surveillance lies in the seductive allure of desire made into wish. This is because in liquid modernity desire is not enough, only wishes that come true will suffice. For the comfortable majority, *normalization* is thus replaced by *precarization*, and when the 'normal' lost its authority, the world became committed, as Bauman might say, on people revealing themselves. In this sense, social control in liquid modernity has for the most part become rather more like the world of Channel 4's *Big Brother*[60] than Orwell's dystopia.

As I have intimated already, for Bauman,[61] the major achievement of the solid modern world underpinned by the Panopticon 'gaze' was its ability to suppress the 'pleasure principle'. For Freud,[62] the 'pleasure principle' is a tendency inherent in the unconscious of all individuals and involves their 'wishes' to seek their own satisfactions regardless of all other considerations. In solid modernity, the suppression of these 'wishes' operated through what Freud called the 'reality principle'. But the price of the triumph of the 'reality principle' was the temporary suspension of the 'pleasure principle', which had to be put off *ad infinitum*. In the event, solid modernity achieved its status quo by 'allowing' its incumbents to achieve the utmost possible expression of their desires with 'normalizing' conditions. Basically, shame was what maintained the 'reality principle': the shame of being found with one's pants down in a compromising situation unworthy of somebody 'normal'. In other words, individuals had to be sure they knew the differences between 'fantasy' and 'reality' in accord with the demands of the 'reality principle'. People were of course wont to take some risks but this did not ultimately ever lead to the complete undermining of the moral order, because with the 'reality principle' intact:

> rather than complete suspension of morality one finds the lifting of the curtain of morals followed by embarrassed or guilty returns to moral codes ... And so the attempt to escape perishes because it depends upon the very conventions that make everyday life possible. By searching for the total sexual encounter, the orgy of freedom and self-expression, the unbridled carnivalesque and the other 'real' experiences which lie beyond civil society, we collide with the antinomies of our desire.[63]

As such, the guiding feature of the 'reality principle' was procrastination. Phillips suggests that desire is the watchword for a society dominated by the 'reality principle', because it is another word for a risk not taken: 'the unlived life that seems the only life worth living'.[64]

The guiding feature of the 'pleasure principle', on the other hand, is instant gratification. As Bauman suggests, liquid modernity is a world where the overriding view is that people must *have* what they desire as a 'wish' and have it now, this very minute. As he adds, the stock in trade aesthetic of consumerism is its ability to abolish delay by taking 'the waiting out of wanting'.[65] If, for Freud, the central goal of life in solid modernity was death, for Bauman, the central goal of life today is to consume. In this sense liquid modernity is the land of fantasy *and* wish fulfilment. Therefore it was inevitable that in a sociality where the individual is first and foremost *homo consumens* that the 'pleasure principle' would come to the fore. Indeed, when the central goal in life is the pleasure of self-indulgence through instant gratification, putting off until later what is presently being denied through the 'reality principle', if not becoming an altogether redundant life-strategy has increasingly been cast in the shadow of the 'pleasure principle'. And when the 'normal' lost its authority, shame, if not disappearing, took on a different but equally meaningful role in people's lives.

Liquid modernity is a world committed, passionate one might say, on people revealing themselves and this is why Bauman understands it as the world of Big Brother Mark Two. With liquid modernity came the individuals' need to shed the burden of their shame, in order to ease the pain: the need to share the anxiety of their distress, to have someone else to carry the burden, not *for* them – in a sociality of individuals that is too much to ask of anybody – but *with* them. This form of confessional is facilitated by the technological advances of the increasingly visual culture of liquid modernity which obliges us to perfom, not just tell, our stories. Here again it is the celebrities, those ubiquitous televisual figures, who perform the central role because their lives make for delicious vicarious reading and what

the avid watchers expect to find in the public confessions of the people in the limelight is the reassurance that their own all-two-familiar loneliness is not just liveable, but given some skill and a modicum of luck may be put to some good use. But what the spectators who eavesdrop on the celebrities' confessions are rewarded with in the first place is the much missed feeling of belonging: What they are promised day by day ('almost any minute of the hour') is a community of non-belonging, a togetherness of loners.[66]

To repeat, with liquid modernity, 'normalization' is thus replaced by 'precarization' as the 'reality principle' and the 'pleasure principle' strike a deal. As Bauman puts it, with liquid modernity it was as if the 'reality principle' and the 'pleasure principle' were destined to make each other's acquaintance, basically because consumer capitalism had on the one hand now found a new way for individuals to share their personal burdens and on the other the market 'needed' them to live out their impulses, irration-alities and perversions. In so doing, liquid modernity marked out that ambivalent territory at the beginning and the end of procrastination. Bauman elucidates:

The two kinds of space … are strikingly different, yet interrelated: they do not converse with each other, yet are in constant communication: they have little in common, yet stimulate similarity. The two spaces are ruled by sharply dissimilar logics, mould different life experiences, gestate diverging life itineraries and narratives which use distinct, often opposite definitions of similar behavioural codes. And yet both spaces are accommodated within the same world – and the world they both are part of is the world of vulnerability and precariousness.[67]

In the event, in liquid modernity the 'solid' conventions of the 'reality principle' are replaced by a 'precarized' hybrid existence far more pervasive, a reality which is paradoxically more intense but at the same time much less sure, less precise than its predecessor – something indefinite, cut into a series of episodes, which is nonetheless sublime in its ephemerality. And what this hybrid world does not share with the imagined worlds of either the 'reality principle' or the 'pleasure principle' is a distinctive singular feel. With the emergence of this hybrid world, people simply began to realize that their most desirable desires are sometimes risks worth taking, worth paying the consequences for.

Liquid modernity: the masturbatory sociality

Bauman does not put it in these terms, but he is essentially arguing that liquid modernity is that stage of history when masturbation came of age. As is well known, in his *History of Sexuality*, Michel Foucault argued that a mounting concern with sex began at the onset of modernity and found its high point in the repressed Victorian era before declining throughout the twentieth century with the emergence of more liberal ways of thinking.[68] As Laqueur[69] has convincingly argued, there were three major reasons why masturbation or what he calls 'solitary sex' was especially derided in solid modernity. First of all, in marked contrast to the social practice of consensual sex between two or more people, masturbation was seen as a 'vice of individuation' which in its climactic moments is a deep and irrevocably private experience. Second, masturbation was understood as problematic because it is a private experience with fantasy rather than a flesh and blood encounter as such and to this extent was never understood as a 'virile act'. Third, and perhaps the most serious worry of all, was the individual's appetite for masturbation, which with its dangerous excesses of self-pleasure was seen as problematic because the individual's urges for it could never be sated. This is because with masturbation comes ambivalence; there is never any satisfaction only an insatiable craving for more.

Liquid modernity is the time when it seems that people have come to terms with masturbation and who would have guessed that its three constitutive features – privacy, fantasy, insatiability – each of which modernity in its formative years taught itself to fear and loathe, would become the watchwords of liquid modernity with its overriding focus on the primacy of the private life of the individual, its relishing of living life as a fantasy and its tacit acceptance of a never-ending cycle of production and consumption: a world in which everybody seems to have access to the boundless excesses of gratification that were once only the rights of a wealthy and privileged minority.

TOWARDS A LIQUID MODERN SOCIOLOGY: OR MOVING BEYOND THE LIMITATIONS OF THE INSIGHTS OF APOCALYPTIC AND INTEGRATED INTELLECTUALS

It is most fitting that the second special case to which Bauman's idea of consumerism will be applied in this chapter, the final section of this book, is intellectual work and specifically the emerging roles of sociologists in liquid modernity. As I demonstrated in Chapter 3, if Bauman's sociology remains true to the idea of praxis, it is also a hermeneutically driven sociology which celebrates the literary basis of the truth claims it makes in its orientation towards grasping the 'mechanism and momentum' of the contemporary world. I also suggested that although Bauman is sociology's biggest fan he thinks that what is most wrong with it today is that it continues to try to make sense of 'society' with the concepts that do not work as well as they once did. But if Bauman is critical of this 'nineteenth-centuryish' sociology, in his more recent work he has also been warning against the kind of sociology that is increasingly coming to replace it and which is 'barely distinguishable from "informed public opinion"'.[70] As Keith Tester has suggested, Bauman is worried that of late 'too many intellectuals have become mere reflections of globalisation and liquidity'.[71]

The argument I develop in this regard suggests that if he once understood intellectual work primarily through the opposition between *legislating* and *interpreting*, Bauman's more recent concern suggests that intellectuals appear to be succumbing to the twin temptations which seduce ordinary men and women in liquid modernity: on the one hand the pop and the pap which inevitably accompanies consumer culture and on the other that of heritage and its accompanying nostalgia, towards which the more disenchanted of liquid moderns tend to make a dash as a political response to the vagaries of consumerism.

Bauman's starting point is that in liquid modernity intellectual work, and by definition sociology, is increasingly divided by these twin temptations. As we have seen already, he suggested in *Legislators and Interpreters* that during the era of 'solid' modernity, intellectuals were needed by the establishment to provide the big ideas to legitimate its power. In his more recent work, however, Bauman suggests that if in liquid modernity intellectual work is generally becoming more interpretive, it is nonetheless marked with a sense of ambivalence because there is a trend in some intellectual work which is not prepared to leave behind its legislative characteristics.[72] In the event, there is a tendency for intellectual work to come in two modes: the 'integrated', which rejects consumer culture out of hand, and the 'apocalyptic', which true to liquid modern form embraces the pop and the pap of consumer culture like there is no tomorrow.[73]

Integrated sociology

According to Peter Beilharz,[74] in much the same way as the legislators, 'the integrated carry on with the tasks of the day, business as usual'. Yet they seldom theorize anew. As Bauman puts it: 'They are more likely to be busy producing and transmitting their own messages, in every sphere, on a daily basis ... the integrated ... are neither pessimists nor optimists (though privately they may be either), but first and foremost they are not dissenters'.[75] In Foucault's meaning,[76] which follows the logic of Nietzsche's genealogy of power relations, integrated intellectuals pretend to be guided by their senses, but they are actually motivated by their ideologies or their martyrs. An aphorism for integrated intellectual activity might be: big ideas may be dead, but let's preserve big ideas.

In sociology the work of the figurationalists[77] reflects the ambivalence associated with integrated intellectual activity. As I have argued elsewhere,[78] the intellectual trajectory of figurationalism is marked by its two historically distinctive roles in sociology. On the one hand, figurationalism can be described as a grand narrative conceived by someone (Norbert Elias) who understood sociological activity as that of a legislating strategy, while on the other it has of late become a type of integrated intellectual activity, maintained by Elias's disciples, such as Eric Dunning and Richard Kilminster,[79] who in their collective output carry forward a self-regulating tradition of sociological thought, merging the first into the second in order to provide a direction for still further expansion of the original grand narrative.

As is well known, figurationalists are sociologists of unswerving faith and share a belief that Norbert Elias, though not infallible, bequeathed them a precious store of permanently valid and reliable 'sensitizing' concepts. This catalogue includes the figuration, interdependencies, process (implicit to this concept is a critique of process reduction), power, involvement and detachment, and of course the centrepiece of it all, the theory of civilizing processes.

As integrated intellectuals, the figurationalists attempt to both defend and transcend the legislating 'perfection' of Norbert Elias's sociology through various stratagems and subterfuges, involving only subtle 'tweaks' to that legislator's work. This is the only way that they can break free from the stultifying influence of the past in order to move their ideas forward. Nowhere is this ambivalence more apparent than in Eric Dunning's book *Sport Matters*. When reading *Sport Matters*, one gets the feeling that Dunning wants to develop his sociological imagination in new directions. Yet the metaphysical structure that he has inherited demands that new ideas must always remain secondary and subservient to the central ideas of Elias. I shall elucidate.

The meaning of Elias's critical distinction between 'involvement' and 'detachment' has long troubled figurational sociology. Despite the implications of some figurational sociologists[80] that Elias uses the term interdependence unconditionally to mean this of independence (detachment) and that of dependence (involvement), numerous authors have criticized this dichotomy in relation to the methodological and epistemological problems associated with 'doing' figurational sociology.[81] Dunning himself acknowledges this problem when he notes that involvement and detachment is 'an area to which figurational sociologists need to devote a great deal more attention'.[82]

Be that as it may, in *Sport Matters* we can see Dunning defending the figurational understanding of the relationship between involvement and detachment by reiterating virulently Elias's key arguments.[83] We can also observe that he seeks to distance himself from the problems associated with this dichotomy by continually evoking the concepts of inter-dependence and *habitus*, particularly in his discussion of gender *habituses* and identities.[84] This type of anxiety continually remains, in Dunning's work, unresolved. In his theoretical discussions, Dunning also skirts very quickly over the concept of the civilizing processes. He continually strives to avoid a reified conception of the civilizing processes by introducing different interpretations of the meaning of the concept, which he hopes will respond flexibly to the demands of each new situation and will anticipate the tendency of non-figurationalists to oversimplify its meaning.

Yet the suspicion is unavoidable that a reified social class hierarchy is always at work in Dunning's thinking regarding this concept. For example, in Dunning, Murphy and Williams's work on football hooliganism,[85] it is obvious that Elias's underlying metaphysics implies that football hooligans will more or less inevitably be rough and working class. Yet more recent work in this area, *vis-à-vis* Bauman's sociology, suggests that such violence is very much contingent upon time and context, rather than being a universal attribute of particular sections of working class men.[86] This work also suggests that despite their efforts to overcome the duality of structure and agency, the figurationalists' synthesis emphasizes similarity rather than difference, fixity rather than contingency: an incongruity that undermines and disrupts the coherent order of the concept of the civilizing process. The figurational approach also relies too heavily on this abstract, reified and logocentric concept of progress, which has little practical content and is difficult to relate to concrete social relations. This gap between theory and 'reality' continually undermines Dunning's attempt to make the theory of civilizing processes relevant to concrete social relations.

Apocalyptic sociology

Whereas the integrated draw their purpose and energies from their martyrs, the apocalyptics not only reject grand narratives but draw their inspiration from the vantage point of the commodified and individualized experience of living in liquid modernity. Moreover, because they are 'free of the immediate need to please their masters, [they] can take more than the occasional snap at the hands that claim to feed them'.[87] Bauman is drawn to apocalyptic intellectual work precisely because it is not tied to any grand narrative. He also knows that any discipline that is out of touch with the world it sets out to represent is in danger of withering away and in this context he is drawn to apocalyptic sociology because not only does it speak the language of liquid modern times, but it always has the potential to fragment, acquire diverse meanings. Indeed, with apocalyptic intellectual work, there always remains the possibility that countering the neo-liberal hegemony can be made conceivable.

However, Bauman also fears apocalyptic intellectual work. His ambivalence towards it owes a great deal to his idea that as much as they are free from the constraints of the ideologies to which the integrated intellectuals are subservient, in a consumer culture the apocalyptic intellectuals are always likely to be 'absorbed' by the dominant neo-liberal hegemony. This is because intellectual lives no longer proceed the same way as before. And the consumerist capitalist economy attempts to abolish intellectualism altogether, mobilizing apocalyptics as consumer guide trainers, experts in anything from football to Big Macs and electronic toys.

Apocalyptic sociology celebrates what the British philosopher Bertrand Russell once called 'useless knowledge': topics which are pleasurable in themselves, but do not present themselves in any way useful. Consequently, this kind of sociology seldom reaches its intended targets. Overdesigned and underwritten apocalyptic sociology is everything that Bauman's sociology is not and it can be seen as a triumph of form over content. In the struggle to hold on to the viewer's attention – apocalyptic sociology is made to be seen rather than read – it has all the cutting-edge carnival of quips and barbs and its protagonists are always ready to connive increasingly melodramatic devices.

Consequently, as in the case of any other commodities purchased on sale, apocalyptic intellectual work is often less than fully honoured; this is because it is always liable to self-commodify. It does not resist the power of the market; it cannot. It does not pretend to be 'outside' consumer culture; it is already inscribed in the flux of that culture, including of course the 'free' market[88] and, equally significant in this process, the mass media. It could not be any other way in 'liquid' modernity. In the event, intellectual work 'becomes televisual. Public intellectuals are televisual intellectuals; they no longer get 15 minutes, only 15 second grabs, and must needs simplify; as well as purring appropriately at the camera'.[89] Bauman suggests that the apocalyptics have been raised on, and numbed by, the altogether less imaginative, less accurate, fabrications of reality that punctuate the television schedules. That the apocalyptics, like the TV schedulers, are obsessed with quick makeover show intellectual work and can be seen appearing on TV 'reality' shows is not unsurprising, because liquid modernity is governed by quick-fix transubstantiations and confessional culture. This televisual culture not only considers that trying to be famous is an intellectual activity but it also ends up treating serious issues lightly and light issues seriously.

Indeed, that apocalyptic sociology expects its legitimacy to be judged by the 'performativity criterion' (to use one of Jean-François Lyotard's terms), inevitably means that its knowledge claims are compelled to be limited and limiting. All that a sociology committed to the 'techniques and technologies' of performativity is capable of producing is the kind of intellectual work that is always trying to be 'bigger' and 'noisier' than that which preceded it. To this extent the sociology of the apocalyptics is crowd-pleasing stuff, it is of the *Hello!* magazine style of criticism and its chief characteristics are populist rather than the subtle food of social observation and critical interpretation. Indeed, all apocalyptic intellectual work has the tawdry taste of comfort cuisine for lovers of Big Macs, albeit prepared by academic chefs: a stodgy 'filling-in' bite, surrounded by the most appetising nuggets, meant to slake the appetite, but it remains ultimately just a 'happy meal' composed of empty intellectual calories.

Apocalyptic and integrated sociology: a summary

In the above discussion we saw that contrary to apocalyptics, for the integrated, the small screen is not the place for learned discussions. We also saw that integrated intellectual work with its *Bildungphilister* attitude is underpinned by a defensive strategy founded in substance over shock. We saw too that the trouble with this strategy is that its narrow-minded intellectualism tends to rely on the heritage ideas of one thinker or one perspective. As a consequence, integrated sociologists are only prepared to read the world in one way which offers images of stability and a sense of continuity in a time of incessant change. Consequently, integrated sociology is only able to aspire to a profoundly conservative vision of what constitutes intellectual work because it relies on clichéd theories and recycled text. It is for all its classical principles proleptic, not least because of its endless reworkings of the same ideas and theories. The integrated might bring new material from other places, but the programmes which they follow and with which they explore these new materials have already been laid out for them in advance. In the event, the integrated have to try hard to find the real-life companions to their sociological narratives.

We saw, too, that integrated sociology may resist the powerful impact of the consumer culture that pervades the works of the apocalyptics, but it is founded on a sensibility that has an inability to handle new vistas and as a result the informational drive of the writing is all too narrowly defined. For all its brio and willingness to acknowledge the shape-shifting qualities of liquid modernity, it merely provides the kind of sociological analyses that feel like a mourning, what Baudrillard might call a fetishism for the lost object.

We saw that the apocalyptics, on the other hand, try to understand the world through the impoverished language-games that consumer culture has trained them in. Accordingly, apocalyptical sociology sacrifices thoughtfulness for pace. By taking a celebrity-magazine approach to sociology, the business of apocalyptic intellectual work is more to do with creating a climate around the work – as well as selling and promoting it – than anything else. Gift-wrapped in Christmas colours, apocalyptic sociology provides a pleasant way of passing the time, but with it there is a desperation to please, to seek the easiest applause and the speediest pay-offs.

However, the bigger problem with these two trends is not just what they imply individually, but, more seriously, what they imply for sociology in relation to each other. What Bauman suggests is the more the apocalyptics immerse themselves in liquid modern capitalist consumer culture the more they deprive themselves of the ability to take a position outside it, whereas the more the integrated deprive themselves of the opportunity to engage with the ideas and theories associated with vocabularies outside their accustomed jurisdiction so they deprive themselves of the opportunity to better grasp the 'progressive individualization of life challenges, the tasks they posit and the responses they call for'.[90] Conjointly these two intellectual strategies fail in their capacity to adequately and responsibly account for the messy realities of human existence and in the event a sociology 'made to the measure' of liquid modernity becomes an impossibility.

A SOCIOLOGY 'MADE TO THE MEASURE' OF LIQUID MODERNITY

Yet all is not lost. We have seen throughout this book that in his own intellectual work, Bauman, in one fell swoop, shatters the sociological lethargy of the integrated at the same time as stirring the stagnant intellectual pond of the apocalyptics. In so doing he effects a passage between the Scylla of the nostalgic and enervating sociology of the integrated and the Charybdis of the topically wide-ranging but analytically anorexic and disappointingly unconventional sociology of the apocalyptics. The reader should have grasped by now that Bauman has forged a unique voice in a world of sociology where, increasingly, bogofs ('buy one get one free' offers) are becoming the *sine qua non* of market success. In a liquid modern world that panders to marketing ideas of what sociology should be like, his instinct is to write against the grain. To use two of his own metaphors, Bauman is no ordinary sociological tourist but a passionate pilgrim, whose work as we have seen throughout this book is chock-a-block with the kind of erudition associated with that of the founding fathers. That said, following Guy Debord's stratagem for analysing the society of the spectacle, Bauman recognizes that to speak of liquid modernity 'means talking its language to some degree'[91] and what this means is that his sociology, unlike that of the integrated, is able to overcome any disdain it has for the extraordinary as well as it is able to reject the 'nineteenth-century' ways of doing sociology which try to keep the subject at the same level. Be that as it may, what Bauman does take from the integrated is that sociology is not all the same, some sociologists are intrinsically better at what they do than others, and it is wrong to pretend any different. He also understands, like the integrated, that it is not cultural up-to-the-minuteness that makes classic sociology but the more elusive element of timelessness. Indeed, as reading Bauman time and again reminds his readers, delight cannot be taught or measured, but good scholarship can.

As I am in the process of finishing writing this book in November 2004, Bauman's prodigious scholarship shows little sign of either retreating from its ability to metamorphose or slowing down. The third book he has published this year,[92] *Europe: An Unfinished Adventure*, which is a brilliant critique of the Hobbesian world Europe seems to have been immersing itself into *ad infinitum* coupled with a political and ethical challenge to its leaders – has just landed on my doorstep. It remains to be seen what Bauman has in store for us as he approaches his ninth decade. *Europe* confirms that this mesmerizing sociologist retains all his powers of witness, of warning and of wonder and we can be sure that whatever it is it will continue to extend the possibilities of the sociological imagination and confirm the truth of one of Bauman's own aphorisms: that 'there is more to what you see and hear than meets the eye, that the most important part is hidden from view, and that there is a huge and dense tissue of inter-human connections below the visible tip of the iceberg. An insight that triggers imagination that, if worked on properly, sediments sociology'.[93]

Suggestions for
Further Reading

It had initially been my intention to provide the reader with an annotated bibliography of all Bauman's major book-length studies, but by the end of the project I decided against this because the primary target of this book is those coming to Bauman for the first time or who need step-by-step guidance.

With these readers in mind, the best place to start is with the interviews, and the pre-eminent and most extensive among these is Z. Bauman and K. Tester, *Conversations with Zygmunt Bauman*, Cambridge: Polity Press (2001), which as well as providing some good background information on the development of Bauman's thought from the early career in Poland right through to the intellectual shift from 'postmodernity' to 'liquid modernity', deals with topics as wide-ranging as ethics and human values, the significance of ambivalence to Bauman's sociology, individualization and consumerism, and politics and justice. For the reader wanting to get a handle on the orientation of Bauman's thinking on liquid modernity, the best interview to consult is Zygmunt Bauman, 'Liquid Sociality', in N. Gane *The Future of Social Theory*, London: Continuum (2004). There are a number of other important interviews which not only provide further insights into Bauman's thought but also enable the introductory reader to better situate him in relation to other thinkers, and in this regard I recommend *The Journey Never Ends: Zygmunt Bauman Talks to Peter Beilharz* and *The Telos Interview* which both appear in P. Beilharz (ed.) *The Bauman Reader*, Oxford: Blackwell (2001); and *Sociology, Postmodernity and Exile: an Interview with Zygmunt Bauman* (with Richard Kilminster and Ian Varcoe) in the appendix of *Intimations of Postmodernity*, London: Routledge (1992).

There is now a burgeoning literature on Bauman's work, and the key texts to which the reader should turn after reading the present book are Peter Beilharz, *Zygmunt Bauman: Dialectic of Modernity*, London: Sage (2000) and Keith Tester, *The Social Thought of Zygmunt Bauman*, Basingstoke: Palgrave MacMillan (2004). Both books are critical but in the main, supportive commentaries which follow Bauman's project, chronologically, from his Marxist beginnings, throughout his postmodern turn to the emergence of liquid modernity, as well as dealing with the major book-length studies. The major difference between the two books is that while Beilharz gives the major studies more individual attention, Tester is more attentive to the literary basis of Bauman's sociology. Dennis Smith's *Zygmunt Bauman: Prophet of Postmodernity*, Cambridge: Polity Press (1999), follows a similar intellectual trajectory, tracing Bauman's writings after the late 1980s with their postmodernist shimmer, but in the process he also places Bauman's work in a dialogue with critical theory and poststructuralism.

Other key resources available to the introductory reader in the secondary literature include the ubiquitous three- or four-page thumbnail sketches usually found in edited collections on social theory (one of the most basically written but also most knowing of these is by Ian Varcoe, which appears in A. Elliott and L. Ray, *Key Contemporary Social Theorists*, Oxford: Blackwell (2003)), and the gargantuan four-volume set *Zygmunt Bauman* (2002) in the *Sage Masters of Modern Social Thought* series, edited by Peter Beilharz.

There is of course no substitute for reading the man himself, and a good starting place is the previously mentioned *Bauman Reader* which is a cornucopia, full of small gems – in part a greatest hits anthology with the interviews thrown in for good measure. Assuming that the reader already has some kind of handle on the ways and means of the sociology from the interviews and secondary literature, the next best place to begin is with the four short volumes published in Polity's *Themes for the 21st Century* series. As its title suggests, *Globalization: The Human Consequences* (1998) deals with the meanings and the consequences of the processes associated with accelerated globalization, but here the reader is also given some first-hand insights into Bauman's aphoristic ability to evoke dualities – the tourists and the vagabonds, global law and local orders – in order to render his arguments both critical and heartfelt. *Europe: An Unfinished Adventure* (2004) is a brilliant critique of the Hobbesian world that Europe seems to have been immersing itself into *ad infinitum*, coupled with a political and ethical challenge to its leaders to stop hanging on to the coat-tails of the USA and find the courage within Europe itself for moving towards a more peaceful integration of humankind in the manner once imagined by Immanuel Kant. The other two volumes, *Identity: Conversations with Benedetto Vecchi* (2004) and *Community: Seeking Safety in an Insecure World* (2001), should be read together and they will enable the reader to get to grips with the two poles between which all Bauman's sociology is strung: freedom and security, individualization and being together.

Besides *Thinking Sociology*, Oxford: Blackwell (1999, 2001), which has as its focus the central task of providing the introductory reader with the ways and means to turn the rhythms of everyday life into an erudite and critical practice that sediments the sociological imagination, the remainder of Bauman's major book-length studies, as I have said already, are in the main difficult to understand because of the intricacy of the ideas, theories, themes and concepts they deal with and on account of their sheer scope, which encompasses a massive range of scholarship from within and without sociology. The best starting point is *Intimations of Postmodernity* which is in effect a collection of already published articles. Though patchwork in its construction, this is Bauman's only real attempt to develop something that might be described as a 'toolkit' sociology, but in saying that, this inclination only really relates to the chapter on 'A Sociological Theory of Postmodernity'. The rest of the book provides one of the most telling discussions ever written of the relationship between postmodernism and sociology and the implications this has for sociological revisionism. The book also contains a gem of a chapter which provides a condensed discussion of Bauman's classic study *Legislators and Interpreters: On Modernity, Post-Modernity and Intellectuals*, Cambridge: Polity Press (1987).

After the preparation suggested above, there should be no problem getting to grips with the rest of Bauman's work; the only real obstacle will be deciding where to begin. As I've intimated throughout this book, Bauman is that rarity, a generalist who extends the power of sociology to create a universe rather than a clique and although he adopts an esoteric perspective, his sociology has the capacity to evoke the full social spectrum of liquid modernity – the worlds of black and white, men and women, rich and poor. A good example of this is *Wasted Lives: Modernity and its Outcasts* Oxford: Blackwell (2004), an amazing feat of empathy, in which Bauman's troubled insight deals with the shock of globalization, environmental pollution and mass displacements. Yet it is the sense of the betrayal of people's lives – in the past, but more particularly in the present – which is the wounded territory of the book.

The reader will find that everywhere in Bauman's work, the metaphorical language is just as superbly judged as the critical engagement with the topic or theme is razor sharp. Whether writing about waste, poverty, consumer culture, community, love or identity, this poet of liquid modernity reminds us what it is like to have been blessed with *sociological imagination*, wide awake to the world as it exists right now. If *Wasted Lives* is an impressive book it is also merely one of the latest instalments in Bauman's impressive project. Sociologists who are serious about their craft owe themselves the pleasure of keeping up with him.

Notes

PREFACE

1 Ulrich Beck, 'Zombie Categories: Interview with Ulrich Beck', in U. Beck and E. Beck-Gernsheim *Individualization*, London: Sage (2002), pp. 202–13, argues that social class has today become a zombie category for a number of reasons which can be identified with processes of individualization, detraditionalization and 'disembedding' in Giddens's meaning.

2 I am indebted to Terry Eagleton, 'Anti-Humanism', in *London Review of Books* (2003), 26(3) 5 February, for this line of argument, who in his review of Amit Chaudhuri's *D.H. Lawrence and 'Difference': Post-Coloniality and the Poetry of the Present*, Oxford: Oxford University Press, provides a critique of the anti-philosopher tradition in modernist thought, extending from Kierkegaard, Nietzsche and Heidegger to Wittgenstein, Adorno, Benjamin, Derrida as well as the work of Richard Rorty.

3 From Karl Marx, *Theses of Feuerbach* (1888), p. xi, quoted in the 3rd edition of the *Oxford Dictionary of Quotations,* Oxford: Oxford University Press (1979).

4   Zygmunt Bauman, *Identity: Conversations with Bendetto Vecchi*, Cambridge: Polity Press (2004), p. 33.
5   Zygmunt Bauman, 'Liquid Sociality', in N. Gane, *The Future of Social Theory*, London: Continuum (2004), p. 22.
6   Zygmunt Bauman, 'Hermeneutics and Modern Social Theory', in D. Held and J.B. Thompson (eds) *Social Theory and Modern Societies: Anthony Giddens and His Critics*, Cambridge: Cambridge University Press (1989), p. 55.

1 AN INTERIM CAREER REPORT

1   Peter Beilharz, 'Editor's Introduction: Bauman's Modernity', in P. Beilharz (ed.) *Zygmunt Bauman: Sage Masters of Modern Social Thought*, London: Sage (2002), p. xxii.
2   Keith Tester, *The Social Thought of Zygmunt Bauman*, Basingstoke: Palgrave Macmillan (2004), p. 137.
3   Zygmunt Bauman, *Legislators and Interpreters: On Modernity, Post-Modernity and Intellectuals*, Cambridge: Polity Press (1987), p. 119.
4   *viz.* Jean Baudrillard, *Simulations*. New York: Semiotext(e) (1983).
5   Gary Genosko, *Baudrillard and Signs: Signification Ablaze*, London: Routledge (1994), p. 36, defines Baudrillard's code as a 'system of rules for the combination of stable sets of terms into messages'. Baudrillard himself would almost certainly describe this attempt to categorize the code as absurd. Indeed, if there are no more agents (subjects), only objects, how can there be any *system* of rules?
6   Jean Baudrillard, *The Mirror of Production*, St Louis: Telos Press (1975), p. 127.
7   Richard Harland, *Superstructuralism: The Philosophy of Structuralism and Post-Structuralism*, London: Routledge (1987).
8   Zygmunt Bauman, *Intimations of Postmodernity*, London: Routledge (1992).
9   Zygmunt Bauman, in Tony Blackshaw, 'Interview with Zygmunt Bauman', *Network: Newsletter of the British Sociological Association* (2002), number 83, October, p. 2.
10 'Liquid Sociality', p. 22.
11 George Ritzer, *Postmodern Social Theory*, London: McGraw-Hill (1997), p. 159.
12 Bauman, *Intimations of Postmodernity*, p. 41.
13 Philip Abrams, *Historical Sociology*, Shepton Mallet: Open Books (1982).
14 Bauman, *Intimations of Postmodernity*, p. 204.

15   Zygmunt Bauman, in Tony Blackshaw, 'Interview with Zygmunt Bauman', p. 3.
16   Ian Varcoe, 'Zygmunt Bauman', in Anthony Elliott and Larry Ray (eds) *Key Contemporary Social Theorists*, Oxford: Blackwell (2003), p. 39.
17   'Hermeneutics and Modern Social Theory', p. 40.
18   Zygmunt Bauman, in Z. Bauman and K. Tester, *Conversations with Zygmunt Bauman*, Cambridge: Polity Press (2001), p. 32.
19   Ian Varcoe, 'Zygmunt Bauman', p. 42.
20   Zygmunt Bauman, 'Foreword by Zygmunt Bauman: Individually, Together', in Ulrich Beck and Elisabeth Beck-Gernsheim (eds) *Individualization*, London: Sage (2002), p. xxii.
21   Zygmunt Bauman, in an interview with Milena Yakimova, 'A Postmodern Grid on the Worldmap', in *Eurozine* (2002) at http://www.eurozine.com/article/2002-11-08-bauman-en.htmtl.
22   Tony Blackshaw, 'The Sociology of Sport Reassessed in Light of the Phenomenon of Zygmunt Bauman', in *International Review for the Sociology of Sport* (2002), 37(2), pp. 199–217.
23   Keith Tester, *The Social Thought of Zygmunt Bauman*, p. 1.
24   Ibid., p. 2.
25   Quoted after James Wood, 'The Slightest Sardine' in *The London Review of Books* (2004), 26(10) May.
26   Charles Wright Mills, *The Sociological Imagination*. Harmondsworth: Penguin (1959).
27   The Research Assessment Exercise (RAE) is a competitive process by which the research performance of United Kingdom university departments is assessed by nominated academics in their subject fields.
28   Bauman, *Intimations of Postmodernity*, p. 190.
29   For a further elaboration on Elias's thought see Robert Van Krieken, *Norbert Elias* (1998) in this series.
30   For a further elaboration on Bourdieu's thought see Richard Jenkins, *Pierre Bourdieu* (second edition), (2002) in this series.
31   Michael Pusey, *Jürgen Habermas*, London: Routledge (1987), p. 26.
32   Anthony Giddens, *New Rules of Sociological Method*. London: Hutchinson (1976).
33   Bauman, *Intimations of Postmodernity*, p. 155.
34   José Guilherme Merquior, *Foucault*, London: Fontana (1987), p. 54.
35   Zygmunt Bauman, *Postmodern Ethics*, Oxford: Blackwell (1993).
36   As Nicholas H. Smith in *Strong Hermeneutics: Contingency and Moral Identity*, London: Routledge (1997), p. 21, points out, drawing

on Charles Taylor's concept of 'perspicuous articulation' in *Philosophical Arguments*, Cambridge: Harvard University Press (1995), 'I have a rational grasp of something if I can articulate it in a perspicuously ordered, *a fortiori* consistent account'.

37   Anthony Giddens, *The Constitution of Society*, Cambridge: Polity Press (1984).

38   'Hermeneutics and Modern Social Theory', p. 55.

39   Zygmunt Bauman, in an interview with Milena Yakimova, 'A Post-modern Grid on the Worldmap', in *Eurozine* (2002) at http://www.eurozine.com/article/2002-11-08-bauman-en.htmtl.

40   Bauman's sociology breaks down all the false dichotomies that continue to nag sociology – between individual and society, fact and fiction, subject and object, and so on and so forth.

41   Bauman, 'A Postmodern Grid on the Worldmap'.

2 BAUMAN'S SOCIOLOGY

1   'Liquid Sociality', p. 17.

2   Robert Rinehart, 'Fictional Methods in Ethnography: Believability, Specks of Glass and Chekhov', in *Qualitative Inquiry* (1998), 4(2), p. 201.

3   For a critical discussion of Bauman's participation in Marxist revisionism see Keith Tester, *The Social Thought of Zygmunt Bauman.*

4   Michel Foucault, 'Preface', in G. Deleuze and F. Guattari (eds) *Anti-Oedipus: Capital and Schizophrenia*, New York: Viking (1983), p. xi (my italics).

5   Frank Parkin, *Max Weber* (revised edition), London: Routledge (2002), p. x.

6   Agnes Heller, *A Theory of Modernity*, Oxford: Blackwell (1999), p. 8.

7   Zygmunt Bauman, *Legislators and Interpreters: On Modernity, Post-Modernity and Intellectuals*, Cambridge: Polity Press (1987), pp. 4–5.

8   Following the lead of Eric Hobsbawm in his seminal history of *The Age of Extremes: the Short Twentieth Century*, where he makes a compelling argument that the 20th century essentially started with the advent of World War One in 1914 and ended in 1991 with the final collapse of the Soviet Union, Arthur Marwick, *The Sixties*, Oxford: Oxford University Press (1998), makes an equally persuasive case for the periodization of the 'long sixties' to be put at between *c.*1958 and *c.*1974.

9   David Macey, 'Zygmunt Bauman', in *The Penguin Dictionary of Critical Theory*, London: Penguin (2000), p. 35.

10 Zygmunt Bauman, *Postmodernity and Its Discontents*. Cambridge: Polity Press (1997), p. 87.

11 In solid modernity, it was indeed within the reach of many to imagine alternative ways of living. Bauman suggests that it is important to acknowledge this, since it would be naive to propose that the denizens of solid modernity were completely embedded – so immersed in their social class and gender positions – that it was impossible for their members to step outside of their *habitus*. Just as they do today, sameness and difference lived side-by-side in solid modernity. It was possible to choose and it was possible to doubt, but for the majority of men and women, in particular the working classes, it was not always that easy because the pressures to conform were strong. In solid modernity, diversity was not the rule of thumb.

12 Keith Tester, *The Social Thought of Zygmunt Bauman*, p. 108.

13 Zygmunt Bauman, 'Britain's Exit From Politics', *New Statesman and Society* (1988), 29 July, p. 36.

14 Ibid.

15 *Identity*, p. 32.

16 Karl Marx, *Capital*, Chicago: Charles H. Kerr and Co. (1906).

17 Harry Harootunian, 'Karatani's Marxian Parallax', in *Radical Philosophy* (2004), 127, p. 31.

18 Walter Benjamin, *The Arcades Project*, Cambridge, MA: Harvard Univeristy Press (1999, 1982).

19 For a brief but full discussion of the major ideas and theorists associated with the Frankfurt School see Tom Bottomore, *The Frankfurt School* (revised edition) (2002) in this series.

20 Theodor W. Adorno and Max Horkheimer, 'Culture Industry: the Enlightenment of Mass Deception', in T.W. Adorno and M. Horkheimer (eds) *Dialectic of Enlightenment*, London: Verso (1979).

21 *Intimations of Postmodernity.*

22 Ibid., p. 188.

23 Zygmunt Bauman, *Identity: Conversations with Benedetto Vecchi*, Cambridge: Polity Press (2004) p. 52.

24 See Slavoj Žižek, *The Sublime Object of Ideology*, London: Verso (1989) and Slavoj Žižek (ed.) *Mapping Ideology*, London: Verso (1994).

25 Mark Poster, 'Critical Theory and Technoculture: Habermas and Baudrillard', in Douglas Kellner (ed.) *Baudrillard: A Critical Reader*, Oxford: Blackwell (1994).

26   Jean Baudrillard, *Paroxysm: Interviews with Phillipe Petit*, London: Verso (1998).
27   *Identity*, p. 74.
28   As Bauman puts it in Daniel Leighton, 'Searching for Politics in an Uncertain World: Interview with Zygmunt Bauman', in *Renewal: a Journal of Labour Politics* (2002), 10(1) Winter: 'In the world of consumers, the poor who are currently un-performing consumer duties are, purely and simply, "flawed consumers" and flawed beyond redemption (and vice versa: those who cannot behave as the right and proper consumer should consider themselves, and are viewed by others, as poor).'
29   Bauman, *Intimations of Postmodernity.*
30   Richard Kilminster and Ian Varcoe, 'Culture and Power in the Writings of Zygmunt Bauman', in Kilminster and Varcoe (eds) *Culture, Modernity and Revolution*, London: Routledge (1996), pp. 215–47.
31   Jean Baudrillard, *The Perfect Crime*, London: Verso (1996).
32   *Identity*, p. 33.
33   *Legislators and Interpreters.*
34   Zygmunt Bauman, *Towards a Critical Sociology: An Essay on Common Sense and Emancipation.* London: Routledge and Kegan Paul (1976).
35   Talcott Parsons, *The Structure of Social Action*, New York: McGraw-Hill (1937).
36   Jean-François Lyotard, *The Postmodern Condition: A Report On Knowledge*, Minneapolis: University of Minneapolis Press (1984).
37   This is not to say that Bauman does not recognize the ambivalence of freedom. For Bauman, freedom is always a social relation rather than an abstract concept and he knows that one person's happiness and freedom can mean another's misery and unfreedom.
38   Isaiah Berlin, *Four Essays on Liberty*, Oxford: Oxford Paperbacks (1969).
39   For a fuller discussion see Henri Lefebvre, *The Sociology of Marx*, New York: Columbia University Press (1982), pp. 5–7.
40   Anthony Giddens, *The Consequences of Modernity*, Cambridge: Polity Press (1990), p. 1.
41   Anthony Giddens, 'Living in Post-Traditional Society', in U. Beck, A. Giddens and S. Lash (eds) *Reflexive Modernization: Politics, Tradition and Aesthetics in the Modern Social Order*. Cambridge: Polity Press (1994), p. 63.
42   Zygmunt Bauman, 'Is there a Postmodern Sociology?', in S. Seidman (ed.) *The Postmodern Turn*, Cambridge: Cambridge University Press (1994).

43 Zygmunt Bauman, *Thinking Sociologically*, Oxford: Blackwell (1990), p. 72.

44 Philip Abrams, *Historical Sociology*, Shepton Mallet: Open Books (1982), p. 93.

45 Dennis Wrong, quoted in Philip Abrams, *Historical Sociology*, pp. 83–4.

46 'Liquid Sociality', p. 20.

47 *Identity*, p. 83.

48 Zygmunt Bauman, in Peter Beilharz (ed.) *The Bauman Reader*, Oxford: Blackwell (2001), p. 164.

49 Ferdinand Tönnies, *Gemeinschaft und Gesellschaft* [Community and Society], London: Routledge (1955, 1887).

50 Jonathan Rée, 'The Brother Koerbagh', in *London Review of Books* (2002), 24(2), p. 21.

51 Agnes Heller, *A Theory of Modernity*, Oxford: Blackwell (1999), p. 7.

52 Zygmunt Bauman, 'Liquid Sociality', in N. Gane (ed.) *The Future of Social Theory*, London: Continuum (2004), p. 20.

53 Cornelius Castoriadis, *The Imaginary Institution of Society*, Cambridge: Polity Press (1987).

54 'Hermeneutics and Modern Social Theory'.

55 Zygmunt Bauman, *Freedom*. Milton Keynes: Open University Press (1988), p. 10.

56 Alan Swingewood, *Cultural Theory and the Problem of Modernity*, Basingstoke: MacMillan (1998), p. 140.

57 Sigmund Freud, 'Civilisation and Its Discontents', published in P. Gay (ed.) *The Freud Reader*, London: Vintage (1995, 1930), p. 725.

58 Ibid., p. 726.

59 Richard Kilminster and Ian Varcoe, 'Culture and Power in the Writings of Zygmunt Bauman', pp. 148–9.

60 Ross Abbinett, *Culture and Identity: Critical Theories*, London: Sage (2003), p. 19.

61 Zygmunt Bauman, *Life in Fragments: Essays in Postmodern Morality*, Oxford: Blackwell (1995), p. 100.

62 Ross Abbinett, *Culture and Identity: Critical Theories*, p. 19.

63 Fordism refers to the methods of organizing mass production most prevalent at the high point of solid modernity and is derived from the manufacturing practices associated with the American car maker Henry Ford. The Holocaust mirrored Fordism in a number of ways, not least through its use of scientific management and large-scale sites for the production of genocide, its rigid production process, and its hierarchal and bureaucratic management structures which drew on both its victims and local unskilled labour for performing

the repetitive and routine tasks needed to keep the production process in motion.

64   Zygmunt Bauman, *Modernity and the Holocaust*, Cambridge: Polity Press (1989, 2000 edition with new Afterword), p. 120.

65   David Macey, 'Zygmunt Bauman', in *Penguin Dictionary of Critical Theory*, London: Penguin (2000), pp. 35–6.

66   I am indebted to Agnes Heller, *A Theory of Modernity*, Oxford: Blackwell (1999), for the metaphor of the railway station and her use of terminology which she draws on brilliantly to distinguish between modernist, unreflected postmodernist and reflected postmodernist sensibilities. In Heller's terminology, Bauman's position is understood as that of a reflected postmodernist.

67   Peter Beilharz, 'Editor's Introduction: Bauman's Modernity', p. xix.

68   Zygmunt Bauman, *Liquid Modernity*, Cambridge: Polity Press (2000), p. 213.

69   Anthony Giddens, *The Constitution of Society*, Cambridge: Polity Press (1984).

70   Zygmunt Bauman, *Modernity and Ambivalence*, Cambridge: Polity Press (1991), p. 272.

71   Max Weber, *The Protestant Ethic and the Spirit of Capitalism*, London: Unwin Hyman (1930).

72   Alexis De Toqueville, quoted in C.B. Welch, *De Tocqueville*, Oxford: Oxford University Press (2001), p. 59.

73   Cheryl B. Welch, *De Tocqueville*, Oxford: Oxford University Press (2001), p. 59.

74   Max Weber, in Frank Parkin, *Max Weber*, p. 30.

75   Frank Parkin, *Max Weber*, p. 32.

76   Zygmunt Bauman, *Mortality, Immortality and Other Life Strategies*, Cambridge: Polity Press (1992), p. 11.

77   Zygmunt Bauman, 'Ziggy in an Age without Stardust', in *The Times Higher* (1998), p. 16.

78   Agnes Heller, *A Theory of Modernity*, p. 6.

79   Anthony Giddens, *Modernity and Self-Identity: Self and Society in the Late Modern Age*. Cambridge: Polity Press (1991).

80   Zygmunt Bauman, in Tony Blackshaw, 'Interview with Zygmunt Bauman', p. 2.

81   Sigmund Freud, *Civilisation and Its Discontents*. Standard Edition xxi: Penguin Freud Library (1930).

82   Ibid.

83   For a fuller discussion see Adam Phillips, 'Bored with Sex', in *London Review of Books* (2003), 25(5), 6 March.

84   Zygmunt Bauman, 'Ziggy in an Age without Stardust', p. 16.

85   Ibid.
86   *Postmodern Ethics*, p. 250.
87   Don Quixote is the chivalrous hero of Saavedra Cervantes's classic
     17th-century book *Don Quixote de la Manche*. Borges's *Pierre
     Menard, Author of Don Quixote* is the story of a minor 20th-century
     author who decided to write his own *Don Quixote de la Manche*, but
     who is able to anticipate many things that Cervantes could not. The
     lesson we learn from Pierre Menard is not only that all powerful
     stories try to claim a special privilege for the worlds they create, but
     also that – to use Bauman's terminology – the legislators told stories
     that were so powerful they came to be seen as something more, as
     unique. After we read *Pierre Menard, Author of Don Quixote*, we
     recognize that the challenge is to tell powerful stories that work
     without claiming such uniqueness or universality.
88   Jean-François Lyotard, *The Postmodern Condition: A Report On
     Knowledge*.

3 THE WAYS AND MEANS OF THE DRAGOMAN

1   Peter Nijhoff, 'The Right to Inconsistency', in *Theory, Culture and
    Society* (1998), 15(1), p. 95.
2   Alan Malachowski, *Richard Rorty*, Chesham: Acumen (2002), p. xii.
3   Anthony Giddens, *New Rules of Sociological Method.*
4   Zygmunt Bauman, 'Hermeneutics and Modern Social Theory', p. 54.
5   Zygmunt Bauman, in Z. Bauman and K. Tester (eds) *Conversations
    with Zygmunt Bauman*, p. 40.
6   See Barney Glaser and Anselm Strauss, *The Discovery of Grounded
    Theory*, London: Weidenfield and Nicholson (1968).
7   For an excellent discussion of the central tenets that both link and
    differentiate the various versions of poststructuralism see Richard
    Harland, *Superstructuralism: The Philosophy of Structuralism and
    Post-Structuralism*, London: Routledge (1987).
8   Richard Rorty, 'The World Well Lost', in *The Consequences of
    Pragmatism*, Minneapolis: University of Minnesota Press (1982),
    pp. 3–18.
9   See Zygmunt Bauman, 'Afterthought: On Writing; On Writing
    Sociology', in *Liquid Modernity*, Cambridge: Polity Press (2000),
    pp. 202–16.
10 Hayden White, *Tropics of Discourse*, Baltimore: Johns Hopkins
    University Press (1978), p. 99.
11 *Modernity and Ambivalence*, p. 272.

12 Angus Bancroft, 'Closed Spaces, Restricted Places: the Resurgence of Politics in the Work of Zygmunt Bauman', in *Zygmunt Bauman: Sage Masters of Modern Social Thought Volume 3*, London: Sage (2000, 2002), p. 61.

13 Richard Rorty, *Contingency, Irony and Solidarity*, Cambridge: Cambridge University Press (1989), p. 9.

14 Bernard Lewis, *From Babel to Dragomans*, Weidenfeld and Nicholson (2004).

15 C. W. Mills, *The Sociological Imagination*, Harmondsworth: Penguin (1959).

16 Peter Beilharz, *Zygmunt Bauman: Dialectic of Modernity*, London: Sage (2000) p. vii.

17 Ibid., p. ix.

18 Samuel R. Delaney, *Silent Interviews: On Language, Race, Sex, Science Fiction, and Some Comics*, Hanover: University Press of New England (1994).

19 See especially *Modernity and Self-Identity: Self and Society in the Late Modern Age*, Cambridge: Polity Press (1991) and *The Transformation of Intimacy: Sexuality, Love and Eroticism in Modern Societies*, Cambridge: Polity Press (1992).

20 Anthony Giddens, *The Transformation of Intimacy*, p. 64.

21 Keith Tester, *The Social Thought of Zygmunt Bauman*, p. 159.

22 Edward Said, 'Thoughts on Late Style', in *London Review of Books* (2004), 26(15), p. 3.

23 I am indebted to John Lanchester for this line of argument which he develops in his excellent discussion of the work of the novelist Muriel Spark. See 'In SparkWorld' in *New York Review of Books* (2004), 60(18), 18 November, pp. 21–4.

24 Keith Tester, *The Social Thought of Zygmunt Bauman*, p. 14.

25 Ibid., p. 16.

26 Milan Kundera, 'Fragments From an Essay: the Theatre of Memory', in *Le Monde Diplomatique* (2003), May.

27 Zygmunt Bauman, *Thinking Sociologically*. Oxford: Blackwell (1990).

28 See in particular Scott Lash, *Critique of Information*, London: Sage (2002).

29 Zygmunt Bauman, *Liquid Modernity*, p. 213.

30 Richard Rorty, in Keith Jenkins, *'What is History': From Carr and Elton to Rorty and White*, London: Routledge (1995), p. 125.

31 Zygmunt Bauman, *Culture as Praxis*, London: Sage (1999), p. l.

32 Richard Rorty, in Steven Connor, *Postmodernist Culture*, Oxford: Blackwell (1989), p. 38.

33 Richard Rorty, *Essays on Heidegger and Others: Philosophical Papers, Volume 2*, Cambridge: Cambridge University Press (1991), p. 19.
34 Nicholas Gane, 'Zygmunt Bauman: Liquid Modernity and Beyond' in *Acta Sociologica* (2001), 44(3), pp. 267–75.
35 'Hermeneutics and Modern Social Theory', p. 55.
36 Jacques Derrida, *Politics of Friendship*, London: Verso (1997), p. 18.
37 Joseph Natoli, *A Primer to Postmodernity*, Oxford: Blackwell (1997), p. 182.
38 See Zygmunt Bauman, *Hermeneutics and Social Science*, London: Hutchinson (1978).
39 Raymond Williams, *Marxism and Literature*, Oxford: Oxford University Press (1977).
40 Austin Harrington, 'Hermeneutics', in A. Harrington, B. Marshall and H.-P. Müller (eds) *Routledge Encyclopaedia of Social Theory*, London: Routledge (forthcoming).
41 *Liquid Modernity*, p. 216.
42 Charles Taylor, *Philosophical Arguments*, Cambridge: Harvard University Press (1995).
43 *Legislators and Interpreters*, p. 5.
44 Ibid.
45 As Martin Heidegger put it in *Being and Time*, Oxford: Blackwell (1962) p. 60, the criticism of the dichotomy between subject and object is plain to see because it is patently obvious that it does not correspond with Dasein and the world.
46 *Intimations of Postmodernity*, pp. 114–48.
47 Zygmunt Bauman, in Tony Blackshaw, 'Interview with Zygmunt Bauman', p. 2.
48 *Intimations of Postmodernity*, p. 42.
49 Raymond Williams, *The English Novel: From Dickens to Lawrence*, London: Chatto and Windus (1970), was concerned with the exploration of the 'knowable community' to unearth 'the substance and meaning of community'. However, he never underestimated the challenge of this task, for he understood that the idea that any community can be known and understood through people and their relationships is always going to complicated.
50 Tony Blackshaw, *Leisure Life: Myth Masculinity and Modernity*, London: Routledge (2003).
51 Ibid., p. 36.
52 Henning Bech, *When Men Meet: Homosexuality and Modernity*, Cambridge: Polity Press (1997), p. 6.
53 Ibid., back board cover.

54   Peter Nijhoff, 'The Right to Inconsistency', p. 93.
55   *Legislators and Interpreters*, p. 5.
56   'Liquid Sociality', p. 23.
57   Keith Tester, *The Social Thought of Zygmunt Bauman*, p. 49.
58   See Zygmunt Bauman, *Socialism: the Active Utopia*, London: Allen and Unwin (1976).
59   *Thinking Sociologically.*
60   David Macey, 'Ostranenie' in *Penguin Dictionary of Critical Theory*, London: Penguin (2000), p. 284. As Macey points out, ostranenie is a Russian term which can be translated as 'making strange' or 'defamiliarization' and is associated with the work of the Russian formalist, Viktor Shklovsky.
61   Where the use of analogy merely asks the reader to think about a particular theme or issue 'as if' or 'as though', Bauman's use of metaphor has a transformative capacity which involves 'seeing as' and in effect forces the reader to defamiliarize the familiar.
62   Henri Lefebvre, *The Sociology of Marx*, New York: Columbia University Press (1982), p. 27.
63   Mary Douglas, *Purity and Danger*, London: Routledge and Kegan Paul (1966).
64   *Culture as Praxis*, pp. 110–11.
65   Ibid., p. 109.
66   *Life in Fragments*, p. 95.
67   *Liquid Modernity*, p. 213.
68   For a discussion of the philosophy of Levinas see Colin Davies, *Levinas: An Introduction*, Cambridge: Polity Press (1996).

4 FREEDOM AND SECURITY IN THE LIQUID MODERN SOCIALITY

1   Zygmunt Bauman, in Tony Blackshaw, 'Interview with Zygmunt Bauman', *Network: Newsletter of the British Sociological Association*, p. 2.
2   *Postmodernity and Its Discontents*, p. 87.
3   *Bildungsroman* is a German noun which is generally used in literary studies to describe a psychological novel. I use it in this context to describe Bauman's work as a psychological sociology.
4   I owe this argument to Iris Murdoch, *Sartre: Romantic Rationalist*, Harmondsworth: Penguin (1987).
5   Karl Simms, *Paul Ricoeur*. London: Routledge (2003), p. 15.
6   It is instructive to recognize that Bauman takes much more from Freud's metaphysics – his theories of modernity – than his psycho-analysis.

7   See especially *Modernity and Self-Identity: Self and Society in the Late Modern Age* and *The Transformation of Intimacy: Sexuality, Love and Eroticism in Modern Societies.*

8   'A Postmodern Grid on the Worldmap'.

9   For further discussion see Arthur C. Danto, *Sartre*, London: Fontana (1975).

10 Benedict Anderson, *Imagined Communities: Reflections on the Origin and Spread of Nationalism*, London: Verso (1983).

11 *Intimations of Postmodernity*, p. 134.

12 *Europe: an Unfinished Adventure*, p. 54.

13 Philip Abrams, *Historical Sociology*, p. 93.

14 *Europe: an Unfinished Adventure*, p. 8.

15 *Postmodernity and Its Discontents*, p. 87.

16 Zygmunt Bauman, 'A Europe of Strangers', *European Synthesis* at http://www.europesynthesis.org (2003), p. 7.

17 Ibid., p. 11.

18 Zygmunt Bauman, in Tony Blackshaw, 'Interview with Zygmunt Bauman', p. 2.

19 Ibid.

20 See, for example, Pierre Bourdieu, *Pascalian Meditations*, Cambridge: Polity Press (2000).

21 Jeremy F. Lane, *Pierre Bourdieu: A Critical Introduction*, London: Pluto Press (2000), p. 194.

22 Ian Varcoe, 'Zygmunt Bauman', in A. Elliott and L. Ray (eds) *Key Contemporary Social Theorists*, Oxford: Blackwell (2003), p. 42.

23 Ibid., p. 193.

24 Ulrich Beck, *Risk Society: Towards a New Modernity*, London: Sage (1992), p. 130.

25 Scott Lash, 'Reflexivity and its Doubles: Structure, Aesthetics, Community', in U. Beck, A. Giddens and S. Lash, *Reflexive Modernization: Politics, Tradition and Aesthetics in the Modern Social Order*, Cambridge: Polity Press (1994), p. 144.

26 Frederic Jameson, 'Postmodernism and Consumer Society', in H. Foster (ed.) *The Anti-Aesthetic*, Port Townsend: Bay Press (1983), p. 119.

27 *Intimations of Postmodernity*, p. 191.

28 Anthony Giddens, 'Living in a Post-Traditional Society, in U. Beck, A. Giddens and S. Lash (eds) *Reflexive Modernization: Politics, Tradition and Aesthetics in the Modern Social Order*, Cambridge: Polity Press (1994), p. 101.

29 *Intimations of Postmodernity*, p. 192.

30 'Foreword by Zygmunt Bauman: Individually, Together', in U. Beck and E. Beck-Gernsheim *Individualization*, p. xvi.

31   Zygmunt Bauman, in Z. Bauman and K. Tester, *Conversations with Zygmunt Bauman*, p. 101.
32   *Intimations of Postmodernity*, p. 27.
33   Ulrich Beck, 'Zombie Categories: Interview with Ulrich Beck', in U. Beck and E. Beck-Gernsheim (eds) *Individualization*, London: Sage (2002), pp. 202–13.
34   Umberto Eco, *Reflections on the Name of the Rose*, London: Secker and Warberg (1986), pp. 557–8.
35   See Erving Goffman, *The Presentation of the Self in Everyday Life*, Harmondsworth: Penguin (1961).
36   *Mortality, Immortality and Other Life Strategies*, p. 184.
37   Ibid.
38   Gilles Deleuze and Felix Guattari, *A Thousand Plateaus*, Minneapolis: University of Minnesota Press (1987), p. 12.
39   'Liquid Sociality', p. 20.
40   *Postmodernity and Its Discontents*, p. 25.
41   *Identity*, p. 32.
42   'Liquid Sociality', pp. 20–1.
43   Ibid., p. 20.
44   Zygmunt Bauman, *Liquid Love*, Cambridge: Polity Press (2003), p. 62.
45   Anthony Giddens, *The Consequences of Modernity*.
46   Dennis Smith, *Zygmunt Bauman: Prophet of Postmodernity*, Oxford: Blackwell (1999), p. 154.
47   Chris Rojek, *Decentring Leisure: Rethinking Leisure Theory*, London: Sage (1995).
48   Zygmunt Bauman, *Community: Seeking Safety in an Insecure World*, Cambridge: Polity Press (2001), p. 1.
49   See, for example, Anthony Cohen's anthropological study, *The Symbolic Construction of Community*, London: Tavistock (1985), which implies that virtually any social group can be understood as a community, potentially and actually. But perhaps the daftest of them all is Jean Baudrillard's discussion in *America*, London: Verso (1989), of the driver community on the Los Angeles freeway system, which is the ultimate illustration of the imagined or imaginary community: a community of those who have no community.
50   The question of community has long troubled sociology. Years before the current fascination with it came about, sociologists were raising doubts about the putative merits of community as a category of analysis. One of the most up-to-date and thoroughgoing discussions which deals with this literature is Gerard Delanty's *Community*, London: Routledge (2003).

51 Paraphrased from Zygmunt Bauman, *City of Fears, City of Hopes*, London: Goldsmiths College (2003), p. 25.

52 The great philosopher George Wilhelm Friedrich Hegel, who was born in Germany in 1770, famously wrote in his book *Elements of the Philosophy of Right*, Cambridge: Cambridge University Press (1991): 'When philosophy paints its grey in grey, a shape of life has grown old and it cannot be rejuvenated, but only recognized, by the grey in grey of philosophy; the owl Minerva begins its flight only with the onset of dusk'.

53 *Community*, pp. 11–12.

54 Barry Wellman *et al.*, 'Networks as Personal Communities', in B. Wellman and S. Berkowitz (eds) *Social Structures: a Network Approach*, Cambridge, Cambridge University Press (1988), p. 134.

55 Michel Maffesoli, *The Time of the Tribes: the Decline of Individualism in a Mass Society*, London: Sage (1996).

56 *Intimations of Postmodernity*, p. 136.

57 Ibid., p. xviii.

58 Zygmunt Bauman, in Tony Blackshaw, 'Interview with Zygmunt Bauman', *Network: Newsletter of the British Sociological Association*, p. 3.

59 *Life in Fragments: Essays in Postmodern Morality*, p. 49.

60 Zygmunt Bauman, 'The Telos Interview', in P. Beilharz (ed.) *The Bauman Reader*, Oxford: Blackwell (2001), p. 21.

61 Raymond Williams, *Keywords*. London: Fontana (1976).

62 *Life in Fragments*, p. 277.

63 Fredric Jameson, 'Pseudo-Couples', in *London Review of Books* (2003), 25(22), November.

64 *Life in Fragments*, p. 277.

65 Ibid., p. 179.

66 Ibid., p. 180.

67 Ibid.

68 Zygmunt Bauman, 'Desert Spectacular', in K. Tester (ed.) *The Flâneur*, London: Routledge (1994), p. 154.

69 Tony Blackshaw, *Leisure Life: Myth, Masculinity and Modernity*, p. 96.

70 It has been argued by Marc Augé in *Non-Places: Introduction to an Anthropology of Supermodernity*, London: Verso (1995), p. 78, that in marked contrast to places (those topographical sites loaded with substance), non-places are merely repositories of liquid flows – what George Ritzer has called nullities – 'which cannot be defined as relational, or historical, or concerned with identity'.

71   John Simmons, *My Sister's a Barista: How They Made Starbuck's a Home Away From Home*, London: Cyan (2004).
72   *Identity*, p. 95.
73   Benedict Anderson, *Imagined Communities*.

5 CONSUMERISM AS THE LIQUID MODERN WAY OF LIFE

1   *Identity*, p. 66.
2   Chris Barker, *Sage Dictionary of Cultural Studies*, London: Sage (2004), p. 33.
3   Steven Miles, *Consumerism as a Way of Life*, London: Sage (1998).
4   *Identity*, p. 91.
5   Richard Harland, *Superstructuralism: the Philosophy of Structuralism and Post-Structuralism*.
6   David Macey, 'Zygmunt Bauman', in *Penguin Dictionary of Critical Theory*, p. 35.
7   'Liquid Sociality', p. 23.
8   *Intimations of Postmodernity*, p. 223.
9   Jean Baudrillard, *In the Shadow of Silent Majorities or, The End of the Social and Other Essays*, New York: Semiotext(e) (1983), p. 46.
10   Zygmunt Bauman, *Freedom*, Milton Keynes: Open University Press (1988), p. 57.
11   *Europe*, p. 94.
12   Ibid.
13   Chris Rojek, *Decentring Leisure: Rethinking Leisure Theory*.
14   *Liquid Love*.
15   Don DeLillo, *White Noise*, London: Picador (1985), pp. 83–4.
16   Jean-François Lyotard, 'Several Silences', in *Driftworks*, New York: Semiotext(e) (1984), p. 109.
17   Linda Grant, 'She's Gotta Have It', in *Guardian G2* (2004), 21 September.
18   Peter Beilharz, 'Editor's Introduction: Bauman's Modernity', p. xxx.
19   *Identity*, p. 75.
20   See especially David Garland, *Punishment in Modern Society: A Study in Social Theory*. Oxford: Oxford University Press (1990).
21   Michel Foucault, *Discipline and Punish: the Birth of the Prison*, Harmondsworth: Penguin (1977).
22   George Orwell, *Nineteen Eighty Four*, Harmondsworth: Penguin (1954).
23   Nico Stehr, 'Modern Societies as Knowledge Societies', in G. Ritzer and B. Smart (eds) *Handbook of Social Theory*, London: Sage (2001), pp. 494–508.

24 Colin Sumner, 'Social Control: the History and Politics of a Central Concept in Anglo-American Sociology', in R. Bergalli and C. Sumner (eds) *Social Control and Political Order*, London: Sage (1997).

25 Tony Blackshaw and Tim Crabbe, *New Perspectives on Sport and 'Deviance': Consumption, Performativity and Social Control*, London: Routledge (2004).

26 Michael Lianos with Mary Douglas, 'Dangerization and the End of Deviance: the Institutional Environment', in D. Garland and R. Sparks (eds) *Criminology and Social Theory*, Oxford: Oxford University Press (2000).

27 *Intimations of Postmodernity*, p. xvi.

28 Ibid., pp. xvi–xvii.

29 *Identity*, p. 52.

30 Zygmunt Bauman, 'Desert Spectacular', in K. Tester (ed.) *The Flâneur*, London: Routledge (1994).

31 *Intimations of Postmodernity*, p. 225.

32 Zygmunt Bauman, *Work, Consumerism and the New Poor*, Buckingham: Open University Press (1998), p. 58.

33 Theodor W. Adorno and Max Horkheimer 'Culture Industry: the Enlightenment of Mass Deception', in T. Adorno and M. Horkheimer (eds) *Dialectic of Enlightenment*. London: Verso (1979).

34 Emma Soames, 'Why 60 is the new middle age ... and 50 is positively youthful', in *Observer* (2004), 1 August.

35 See especially Zygmunt Bauman, *In Search of Politics*, Cambridge: Polity Press (1999).

36 *Work, Consumerism and the New Poor*, p. 31.

37 Jean Baudrillard, *America*. London: Verso (1989), p. 35.

38 Pyotr Chaadaev quoted after Pankaj Mishra 'Introduction', in V.S. Naipaul (ed.) *Literary Occasions: Essays*. Basingstoke: Pan Macmillan (2003), pp. vii–viii.

39 Antoine de Saint-Exupéry was a writer and a French pioneer aviator, who disappeared on a wartime mission over occupied France.

40 Quoted after James Fenton, 'Something of the Night ...', 'Dispatches', in *Guardian Review* (2004), p. 28.

41 Zygmunt Bauman, in Daniel Leighton, 'Searching for Politics in an Uncertain World: Interview with Zygmunt Bauman', in *Renewal: A Journal of Labour Politics* (2002), 10(1), Winter.

42 *Identity*, p. 74.

43 Theodor W. Adorno, *The Culture Industry: Selected Essays on Mass Culture* (edited), London: Routledge (1991).

44 Jürgen Habermas, *Legitimation Crisis*, London: Heinemann Educational Books (1976).

45 *Intimations of Postmodernity*, pp. 97–8.
46 Anthony Giddens, *Modernity and Self-Identity: Self and Society in the Late Modern Age*.
47 *Intimations of Postmodernity*, p. 98.
48 Ibid., p. 98.
49 M. Feeley and J. Simon, 'The New Penology: Notes on the Emerging Strategy of Corrections and its Implications', *Criminology* (1992), 30(4), p. 452.
50 Zygmunt Bauman, in Daniel Leighton, 'Searching for Politics in an Uncertain World: Interview with Zygmunt Bauman'.
51 *Life in Fragments*, p. 100.
52 Keith Tester, *The Social Thought of Zygmunt Bauman*, p. 127.
53 Ibid., p. 98.
54 Thomas Mathiesen, 'The Viewer Society: Michel Foucault's "Panopticon" Revisited', in *Theoretical Criminology* (1997), pp. 215–34.
55 *Work, Consumerism and the New Poor*, p. 53.
56 Debord suggested that the spectacle is all there is – even if most 'spectacles' are nothing more than tacky commercial stunts, shadowlike non-events, dressed up like the 'real' thing, but merely manufactured with profit in mind.
57 Nicholas Bouuriaud, quoted in Hal Foster, 'Arty Party', in *London Review of Books* (2003), 25(23).
58 Anushka Asthana, 'I Want to Be Beyoncé (or Thierry Henry)', in *Observer* (2004), 19 December.
59 See Richard Schickel, *Common Fame: the Culture of Celebrity*, London: Pavilion Books (1985). This myth of celebrities hanging around together is very well depicted in one of 2DTV's most popular comedy sketches which has as its focus the shared world of Elton John, George Michael and Geri Halliwell.
60 Channel 4's *Big Brother* is a 'reality' game television programme which is based on the Darwinian idea of the survival of the fittest. It is a game in which the contestants are one by one eliminated from the *Big Brother* 'house' by a voting audience. As a result the contestants are first and foremost competitors who on the one hand scheme against each other in order to avoid elimination but on the other try to convince the audience why they should not be voted off the show by revealing their 'authentic' selves (*sic*) through a kind of public confessional.
61 Zygmunt Bauman, *Society Under Siege*, Cambridge: Polity Press (2002).

62   Sigmund Freud, *Beyond the Pleasure Principle*, London: Hogarth Press (1920).

63   Chris Rojek, *Decentring Leisure*, p. 88.

64   Adam Phillips, 'Bored with Sex', in *London Review of Books* (2003), 25(5), 6 March, p. 9.

65   *Liquid Modernity*, p. 159.

66   *Community*, pp. 67–68.

67   *Liquid Modernity*, p. 160.

68   Michel Foucault, *The History of Sexuality: An Introduction*, Harmondsworth: Penguin (1978).

69   Thomas Laqueur, *Solitary Sex: A Cultural History of Masturbation*, New York: Zone Books (2003).

70   'Hermeneutics and Modern Social Theory', pp. 54–5.

71   Keith Tester, *The Social Thought of Zygmunt Bauman*, p. 180.

72   Zygmunt Bauman, *In Search of Politics*, Cambridge: Polity Press (1999).

73   In making these arguments, Bauman draws on the work of Umberto Eco in 'Apocalyptic and Integrated Intellectuals', in R. Lumley (ed.) *Apocalypse Postponed*. Bloomington: Indiana University Press (1994).

74   Peter Beilharz, *Zygmunt Bauman: Dialectic of Modernity*, p. 166.

75   *In Search of Politics*, p. 101.

76   Michel Foucault, 'Truth and Power', in C. Gordon (ed.) *Michel Foucault: Power/Knowledge*, Hemel Hempstead: Harvester (1980).

77   Figurationalism or Eliasian sociology, as it is also known, has its origins in the work of Norbert Elias. For a full discussion see Robert Van Krieken, *Norbert Elias* (1998) in this series.

78   Tony Blackshaw, 'The Sociology of Sport Re-assessed in the Light of the Phenomenon of Zygmunt Bauman', in *International Review for the Sociology of Sport* (2002), 37(2), pp. 199–217.

79   See especially Eric Dunning, *Sport Matters: Sociological Studies of Sport, Violence and Civilization*, London: Routledge (1999) and Richard Kilminster, *The Sociological Revolution: From the Enlightenment to the Global Age*, London: Routledge (1998).

80   Thomas Scheff, 'Unpacking the Civilizing Process: Shame and Integration in Elias's Work' (1997), at http://shop.usyd.ed.au/su/social/elias/confpap/scheff2.htm (17 February 2000).

81   See especially Derek Layder, 'Social Reality as Figuration: a Critique of Elias's Conception of Sociological Analysis', *Sociology* (1986), 20(3), pp. 367–86; Chris Rojek, *Capitalism and Leisure Theory*, London: Tavistock (1985); Chris Rojek, 'The Problems of Involvement and Detachment in the Writings of Norbert Elias', *British Journal of Sociology* (1986), 37(4), pp. 584–96; and Chris Rojek,

'The Field of Play in Sport and Leisure Studies', in E. Dunning and C. Rojek (eds) *Sport and Leisure in the Civilizing Process: Critique and Counter-Critique*, London: Macmillan (1992).

82 Eric Dunning 'Figurational Sociology and the Sociology of Sport', in E. Dunning and C. Rojek (eds) *Sport and Leisure in the Civilizing Process: Critique and Counter-Critique*, London: Macmillan (1992), p. 254.

83 Ibid., pp. 243–6.

84 Ibid., pp. 221–9.

85 Eric Dunning, Patrick Murphy and John Williams, *The Roots of Football Hooliganism*, London: Routledge (1988).

86 See, for example, Gary Armstrong, *Football Hooligans: Knowing the Score*, Oxford: Berg (1998) and Gary Robson, *'No One Likes Us, We Don't Care': the Myth and Reality of Millwall Fandom*, Oxford: Berg (2000).

87 Peter Beilharz, *Zygmunt Bauman: Dialectic of Modernity*, p. 166.

88 Joseph Natoli, *A Primer to Postmodernity*.

89 Peter Beilharz, *Zygmunt Bauman: Dialectic of Modernity*, p. 166.

90 'A Postmodern Grid on the Worldmap'.

91 Guy Debord, *The Society of the Spectacle*, New York: Zone Books (1995), Thesis 11.

92 Four books if you include the second edition of *Work, Consumerism and the New Poor* (2004).

93 Zygmunt Bauman, in Tony Blackshaw, 'Interview with Zygmunt Bauman', October, p. 1.

Index